Lived Experience Phenomenon
Teaching Methods

Ana Harvey & Marcia Roy

Cover image © Shutterstock.com

www.kendallhunt.com
Send all inquiries to:
4050 Westmark Drive
Dubuque, IA 52004-1840

Copyright © 2017 by Kendall Hunt Publishing Company

ISBN: 978-1-5249-2180-4

All rights reserved. No part of this publication may be reproduced,
stored in a retrieval system, or transmitted, in any form or by any means,
electronic, mechanical, photocopying, recording, or otherwise,
without the prior written permission of the copyright owner.

Published in the United States of America

CONTENTS

CHAPTER 1 – THE BIG PICTURE   1

Lived Experience Phenomenon (LEP) Defined   2
LEP and Inquisitive Reflection   4
Why Use LEP Teaching Methods?   7

CHAPTER 2 – PRECOURSE PREPARATION   15

First Impressions: Setting the Tone for LEP   16
Mindshift from Content Absorption to Content Connection for
    Memory Retention   20
LEP Mind Mapping and the Role of the Educator   23

CHAPTER 3 – TIME FOR ACTION   29

LEP Mindful Engagement   29
Infusing LEP in the College Classroom through Memory Systems   30
    Working with Memory   31
    LEP and Short-Term Memory   34
    LEP Long-Term Memory   36
        LEP and Explicit Memories   36
        LEP and Implicit Memories   38
        Procedural Memories   38
    Priming and Conditioning   39
    Triggers and Memory Retrieval   42

CHAPTER 4 – IT'S PERSONAL: INFUSING LEP INQUISITIVE REFLECTION TO LEARNING   43

Infusing LEP Inquisitive Reflection to Critical Thinking   44
Transforming LEP Inquisitive Reflection to Authentic Learning   46
LEP Oral Instruction, Writing, and Journaling   48
    Oral Instruction   48
    LEP Writing   50
    Journaling   52

CHAPTER 5 – IT'S PERSONAL: LEP PROBLEM SOLVING   55

LEP Problem Solving through Creative Visualization   58
Creating Transformative Meaning through LEP's Inquisitive Reflection   60

CHAPTER 6 – IT'S PERSONAL: KNOWLEDGE ACQUISITION THROUGH INFORMATION SEEKING   63

LEP and Learning Styles   64
Infusing LEP through Content, Story, Discussion, Group Work and Blogs   66
    Content   66
    Story   66
    Discussion   67
    Group Work   68
    Blogs   70

CHAPTER 7 – IT'S PERSONAL: IMPLICATIONS FOR ONLINE LEARNING   73

Organizing Online Learning Platform to Include LEP   74
Addressing Feedback to Online Students   77

CHAPTER 8 – CULTURAL AWARENESS IN TEACHING AND LEARNING 79

Coining a Culturally Diverse College Classroom 80
Cultural Variations in Learning Patterns 82

CHAPTER 9 – MOVING BEYOND TRADITIONAL TEACHING 85

Reframing Education through LEP Teaching Methods and Exploring the Possibilities 86
Building the Next Generation of LEP Educational Leaders 88

CHAPTER 10 – ASSESSMENTS 91

LEP and Tests 94
LEP Assessment Examples 95

CHAPTER 11 – INSTRUCTIONAL MIND MAPPING ACTIVITIES AND HELPFUL HANDOUTS 105

Instructional Mind Mapping Activities and Helpful Handouts 105

References *123*

CHAPTER ONE

THE BIG PICTURE

LIVED EXPERIENCE PHENOMENON (LEP) DEFINED
LEP AND INQUISITIVE REFLECTION
WHY USE LEP TEACHING METHODS?

"The goal is to provide inspiring information that moves people to action."

—Guy Kawasaki

Speak to the mind. Lived Experience Phenomenon (LEP) has emerged as an authentic highly successful teaching method which significantly increases student engagement, in school retention, learning outcomes and long term memory retention because it speaks to the mind. The power of the LEP teaching method is in its ability to tap into the memories (lived experiences) of students and create connections between these memories and new information to assist in learning and memory retention. At the heart of the LEP teaching method lies "LEP's inquisitive reflection" which allows for a mind shift from "content absorption" to "content connection" and authentic understanding and learning of new information in a very personal way, unique to each student.

The objective of this book is to provide a successful adaptable teaching tool for educators to use to engage students in opening their minds to an innovative learning process, the LEP teaching method, which utilizes LEP's inquisitive reflection as an intentional instructor design to significantly enhance the learning environment. Further, the intention is to share with educators for food for thought, and practical applications, the use of LEP in the college classroom, either face to face or via technology, where students feel a part of the learning process and mind maps unfold not only for the learner but also for the teacher. It is often said that life is a journey. Why not then delve into that journey, in a personal way in the classroom, so that lived experiences are highlighted rather than ignored, creating a space within a learning environment where personal knowledge becomes not only relevant but a useful instrument to assist in the understanding and retention of new learning.

LIVED EXPERIENCE PHENOMENON (LEP) DEFINED

> *"Everyone has their own different life experiences which make them who they are. No two people's life experiences are the same. And mine are just unique to me."*
>
> —Keshia Knight Pulliam

The terminology of "lived experiences" may sound rather strange, as it almost appears as tautological. What can an experience be if it is not lived? Does just breathing constitute a lived experience if there isn't any meaning? Schutz (1967, p. 69-71) contends that "meaning does not lie in the experience. Rather those experiences are meaningful which are grasped reflectively. It is then incorrect to say that my lived experiences are meaningful merely in virtue of their being exercised or lived through. The reflective glance singles out an elapsed lived experience and constitutes it as meaningful." This means that the meaning of the experience is essentially something constructed; it lies in what is made of …what is lived through (Schutz, 1967) that makes it significant. Schutz (1967) further notes that the full meaning of experience is not just the immediacy of the lived moment, but it emerges from explicit retrospection where meaning is recovered and reenacted. Past lived experiences that have not been categorized cannot serve as a basis for comprehension and understanding of new information. The lived experiences must be organized in the mind and assigned meaning for understanding and learning to occur.

Lived experiences are accessed through memory. Lived experiences, in essence, are meaningful memories of individuals' lived history. They are comprised of constructs that are organized based on previous experiences and include various temporal and spatial organizations that in simplistic form involve immediate consciousness of life preceding reflection (Dilthey, 1985; Sartre, 1957). Denzin (1992) contends that lived experience exists only as a representation and does not exist outside of memory.

The relationship between memory and lived experience is at the center of LEP learning. Memory is an active process, and people choose what to remember and how they represent those memories. The ways individuals choose to remember is a cognitive, social and emotional process in which construction of memories (lived experiences) is an ongoing process. But it is important to note that the practice of memory construction is imaginative (Denzin, 2001) because people choose what to remember; thus, memory may not be credible. Since memories are just representations and not the factual events, often memories of lived experiences are biased because the individual's subconscious mind uses a lens that sees life from a personal perception, which is usually curved to their advantage, thus "elaboration and invention are common traits of ordinary remembering" (Bartlett, 1932, p. 205). Moreover, recollection is not merely reduplicative but is socially influenced (Bartlett, 1967). That is people engage in memory making processes in which the individuals' lived experiences often reflect their social constructs that shape their memories (Barkley, 2008).

Memories are not just recalling facts but are filtered through sharing perceptions about those facts. Thus, because personal perception has now infiltrated the facts, the possibility of describing the lived experience with great precision and recalling every moment accurately is not usually possible or achieved by people when recalling information. However, when learning new material it may not necessitate that the individual remember actual facts of events or situations, because memory, accurate or not, can still be used as a point of reference for understanding. A memory, true or not, can always be manipulated by the rememberer to explain and frame new information and assign it meaning. When a memory is framed within the individual's existing knowledge, it now has meaning and can be integrated with new information which will bring about new knowledge. It is through assimilation of old and new memories that knowledge is formed.

In order to better understand the lived experience phenomenon, sociology of emotion must be included in the paradigm. Denzin (1985) referred to the two modes of lived experience as feeling the lived experience, and feelings while telling about them. He viewed these as lived body, and intentional value feelings, respectively. Feeling the lived experience is connected to formalizing emotions to the memory, and feelings associated with the telling of lived experience "are felt reflections, cognitive and emotional, about feelings" (Denzin, 1985, p. 230); thus the second level of emotions is the result of reflecting on our experiences and placing an importance on the feelings associated while telling about the experience. Feelings associated with the lived experience often are more important and more telling than the event itself. These memories and feelings are available and students can tap into this unexplored well of knowledge to use for exploration, content connection, and as a memory reinforcement of new knowledge and learning.

Feelings of lived experiences are directly related to perception. Perception is directly related to learning. It is important that educators do not just focus on the event of the *lived experience* itself, but also give emotions and feelings associated with the lived experience proper consideration. This will motivate students to dig deeper within their own memories, increase growth within the students and assist in the memory retention of content under study.

The students' classroom reality and specifically their lived experiences while learning must be positive in order for student engagement and in-school retention to occur. The students lived experiences must include the current structure of learning such as lecture, textbooks, theories, memorization, and so on. However, research in student engagement and retention shows that this is not enough and that very often students cannot learn and retain information long term in this linear way. Introducing LEP into the curriculum will spark a new level of interest, allow students to consistently accrue new information in a very personal way and tap into their great inner wisdom of their own lived experiences to assimilate, expand their knowledge and increase their memory retention. In today's world students need to take a step back from technology as their first choice for information and plug in their efforts into their own inner super highway of lived experiences that are just waiting to be retrieved and used.

LEP AND INQUISITIVE REFLECTION

> *"Without reflection, we go blindly on our way, creating more unintended consequences, and failing to achieve anything useful."*
>
> —Margaret J. Wheatley

Reflecting in its simplistic terms means looking back into the past. LEP's inquisitive reflection involves directed investigative inquiry of lived experiences as it applies to content under study, while looking back. Students are people who are busy with their lives and very few students view their lived experiences as important happenings and opportunities for learning. Psychologists refer to this type of life perception as "episodic grasp of reality" (Feuerstein, 1980). This is not how we want students to live or learn. Students should get into the habit of connecting and constructing meaning from their lived experiences, and to do that they must use LEP and the art of inquisitive reflection. (LEP's inquisitive reflection mind mapping (see Activity 1) is designed to specifically engage students' brain for optimal learning outcomes and make the material learned real and memorable. As with all mind mapping exercises, it must be customized for specific concepts and discipline). Teachers who endorse LEP classrooms ensure that students are fully engaged in inquisitive reflection and meaning making that can easily be applied to concepts taught and thereby expanding understanding and assisting in the long-term memory retention process.

Within the LEP method teaching students how to reflect is of utmost importance. Reflection is a means to discover and transform understanding (Mezirow, 1990). It is an exploration and explanation of data in a mind. Reflecting is deliberate and structured in thinking, but reflections are not merely descriptions of how good or bad an experience was; instead in reflection students must consider what was learned from the experience and how it ties into the concepts being learned. Costa and Kallick (2008) affirm the importance of educators monitoring students' progress and contend that educators must assist students to construct meanings from the concepts learned and show them how the learning applies to other contexts or settings through the use of self reflection. In this way learning is interesting, enjoyable and increases the chances of long-term memory retention. Moreover, learning becomes a continual process of *engaging* the mind that *transforms* the mind (Costa & Kallick, 2008).

The Five Phases of Reflection as exemplified by Harris et al. (2010) is in line with LEP's inquisitive reflection as it is applied to learning. Harris et al. (2010) contend and LEP teaching methods demonstrate that the active reflective process requires movement in and out of the various phases.

- **DESCRIPTIVE PHASE:** Students at the descriptive phase have limited perceptions relating to new information or concepts under study. Concepts are simply described in a reporting manner such as the textbook interpretation of the concept. At this phase educators should clarify the concepts as much as possible through framing, lecture, priming, discussion, reading assignment and other modes to introduce and frame the concept for the student.

- **INQUISITIVE PHASE:** In this phase of inquisitive thinking students begin to search their memories, knowledge, and lived experience in order to frame and formulate an understanding of the concept through existing memories. At this phase educators should assist students to search their memories to construct a connection between content and the associated memory.

- **INVESTIGATIVE PHASE:** Students in the investigative phase are able to identify memories of lived experiences that connect to the concept. Students begin to form an understanding of the concept and are able to draw on its meaning. At this phase the educators should assist the students to draw meaning from the concept learned to the best of their ability.

- **INTERDEPENDENT PHASE:** Students in the interdependent phase are easily able to connect to past experiences and can apply theory to practice. Students at this phase have full understanding of the concept and can see how the concept operates in their life. Additionally, students identify a trigger to use as a cue to recall the information when needed. At this phase, the educators monitor the students' progress; assist in identifying triggers, and assists when needed.

- **GLOBAL PHASE:** Students in the global phase consider how the content under study operates in a more global setting. Based on knowledge and lived experiences, students begin to see the inter-connectedness of what they are learning and how it will serve them, not only personally, but in the world at large. Educators at this phase continue to monitor and be a support system to students assisting only when needed.

Reflective thinking in learning is critical. Reflective thinking in learning is so important that Charner-Laird et al. (2003, p. 9) describe reflective thinking as the "mind's strongest glue for making the connections necessary to understanding, regardless of content." But in order for students to master the LEP inquisitive reflection process, they must be given ample opportunity to practice using their reflective skills. The included LEP inquisitive reflection/critical thinking skills activity (see Activity 2) and the suggested LEP in-class short exercises (see Activity 3) will assist students to practice the art of reflection. Students should be encouraged to practice their LEP inquisitive reflection skills often, as the more they practice, the greater their skills and results in comprehension of concepts and better memory retention.

WHY USE LEP TEACHING METHODS?

> *"We shall not cease from exploration and the end of all our exploring will be to arrive where we started and know the place for the very first time."*
>
> —T.S. Eliot

From memories comes much understanding. T.S. Eliot noted that "what we call the beginning is often the end... The end is where we start from." When working with LEP and memories, the end is where the students' learning starts. Revisiting memories may be at times, emotional, painful, uncomfortable, or joyful, but it is always enlightening in terms of understanding and new knowledge. Students have the power within their memories to return to their past experiences in their minds. Just as Eliot indicated, and "know the place for the very first time" because now they see and move through these experiences with fresh eyes, and can use these memories, these past experiences, whether perceived as good or bad, for new learning and to their greatest advantage. Memories are no longer something that is buried in the students mind never to see expression, but an active, engaging and effective tool for learning.

Memories of lived experiences are humanity's greatest teacher because it directly affects how we learn, see, and understand the world. Within each of us there is a unique mind composed of a warehouse of memories that often lay dormant, especially in the college environment where students grapple with visualizing the connections of what they know and have experienced, as aligned to their academic discipline. The adages "Why do I have to learn this?" and "What does this have to do with me?" ring especially true in the college classroom where students are embarking upon an educational path toward an academic and career goal, a choice they have made for their work and life beyond college.

Engaging these students genuinely in the course content of a particular discipline is a challenge for all educators as students see college courses as a requirement for their major, a hurdle to cross to get someplace else. How can educators bridge this disinterest and help their students see the linkage between the value of what they are learning, their daily lives and future potential? How do educators engage the minds of their students and help them see the purpose and meaning of learning? LEP teaching method assists in answering these questions and provides fascinating results because it has the potential to help students learn, stay engaged for the duration of the course, and retain new information in the long term.

Student engagement leads to student retention and is one of the most monumental challenges in higher education universally. From the college and university perspective, low graduation and completion rates often greatly affect institutions' bottom line and academic standings. Educators are concerned about this phenomenon and often feel lacking in their own abilities to affect change. The higher education landscape can be frustrating in its complexity, and retaining students and increased degree completion rates are complex issues that all higher education institutions face. And, we ask ourselves, as college educators, what can we do? How can we make a difference in this landscape? What do we have to offer to do our part so that students feel connected to their learning and see the relevance of what they are studying to their eventual career or life goals? As educators we strive to address these issues by developing new programs and new strategies that are dynamic and effective enough to change this current negative student retention trend; however, current college dropout statistics in 2015 indicate that 30% of college and university students drop out after their first year and 70% of Americans will study at a 4-year college, but less than two-thirds will graduate (CollegeAtlas, 2015).

To increase retention rates, students must be actively engaged in the learning process; there is no way around that. Students who are engaged in their college classrooms are active learners and can then "make an idea, a concept, or a solution their own by working it into their own personal knowledge and experience" (Barkley, 2010, p. 16). And although traditionally student engagement is defined as "students' academic commitment and application," student engagement is not the sole responsibility of the student because it includes interacting in a learning environment (Astin, 1984; Bryson & Hand, 2007) guided by the educator as the lead. Educators who provide an optimal learning setting in which to facilitate the lesson for meeting the course and student learning outcomes realize that student engagement is critical and must find ways to accomplish this goal.

LEP enhances the engagement level of the college classroom to a marked degree by immersing students in authentic learning that is meaningful to them. This immersion influences retention and degree attainment positively, leading to students completing their academic goals, which can, in turn, provide both an emotional and a financial gain that are added incentives for students to remain in school. Research unequivocally contends that college credentials improve a person's earning potential (United States Department of Labor, Bureau of Labor Statistics, 2016). Students, parents, and society understand and know this. And while we could dismiss students' disinterest or apathy in our college classrooms to a responsibility on the part of the student to address, college-level educators everywhere must do their part if we want our students to remain in our classes.

While incredibly talented in their subject disciplines and knowledgeable in great depth as to what to share, educators are often challenged with how to create those bridges of engagement for their students. Chen and Peng (2008) indicate that academic success is more than acquisition of knowledge and that the classroom is a vital introductory point for helping students to begin to master the material learned. In support of this, Meyer and Land (2005) assert that the classroom needs to include active and interactive learning. Thus, it is not enough to speak of engagement and the importance of connecting our students to learning in our college classrooms, but innovative action has to be taken and concerted efforts must be made to make a positive difference on retention and degree attainment at our higher education institutions. Through experimenting with new and innovative teaching and learning approaches such as LEP teaching method, educators can increase student engagement, retention and learning outcomes in their classrooms.

The consequences of not having a plan to engage students in learning are grim (Claxton, 2007). "Some educationists consider engaging disengaged pupils to be one of the biggest challenges facing educators, as between 25% (Willms, 2003) and over 66% (Cothran & Ennis, 2000) of students are considered to be disengaged" (as cited in Harris, 2008, p. 57). Student engagement and retention largely depend on each other, as students must be engaged if they are to be retained. Students who are engaged are less likely to drop the course, are present in mind and body, have a higher self-esteem and confidence of the material, enjoy the course and are much more likely to complete it.

There are a number of valid and practical ways to address student engagement and retention in higher education institutions from increasing advisor tracking of at-risk students, adding tutoring and support systems, mentoring, among others. However, significant statistics that continue to show negative retention and degree attainment trend by students nationwide indicate that these efforts are not enough and that fresh approaches, such as the LEP teaching method, that stretches beyond the building blocks of learning knowledge and remembering facts for the short term are needed, and needed now. Why LEP? Because LEP gets personal and defines the concepts under study from a personal outlook and sets the tone of "there is something in this for me" which increases student engagement leading to increased retention.

Igniting the minds of students to bring forth their stored memories to connect to the content taught through inquisitive reflections of LEP is a fascinating teaching method that can supplement any teaching style, in a wide variety of disciplines, and can embrace many different student learning styles in the process. LEP has the capacity to stand alone, but its applications' uniqueness lends itself to be modified across many teaching styles, methods, practices, approaches and disciplines. LEP teaching methods produce immediate results in increased student engagement leading to increased critical thinking skills in a personal manner, increased application of personal meaning through reflection, and increased long-term memory of concepts.

LEP learning is applicable to every student because everyone has a mind that consists of their narrative; everyone learns through stories and learns with their special kind of personal perception. That perception is different in each individual, even though the experience/event might have been similar because introspections, thoughts, feelings, perceptions, observations and critical thinking processes are unique, as each person is unique; thus the same event can be viewed very differently depending on the perception of the individual. Pink (2005) speaks of human beings as possessing two minds, two broad areas of cognition processing; and terms that the left and right brain are becoming more and more commonly recognized as having distinctively different attributes: the left more reason and analysis, the right more holistic and emotional (Pink, 2005). But, while Pink (2005) makes many strong points for a consideration of the importance of lived experiences through his various and diverse analogies, he uses the term "meaning maker" as exemplifying someone who has the prospect of a more flourishing future, proposing as he does that "the keys to the kingdom are changing hands."

Translate this to the college classroom, and educators are challenged with the notion of creating meaning within their discipline contexts, helping students become these meaning makers that Pink (2006) emphasizes as being important for a developing global society. This translation is a struggle for many well-informed college educators who know and love their subjects but have angst with the bridging of the discipline knowledge to their students' abilities to process information in a manner of personal relevance. Utilizing practices of LEP can provide the bridge, that opening so needed in helping students make meaning of something they know well: their own lived experiences. Educators must recognize that each student is operating from a different motivational drive, but that all students come to a college classroom with skill sets and knowledge from their lived experiences that they can tap into and use as a personal resource.

Incorporating LEP within the college classroom as a vehicle of engagement, designed within the lessons of the college class that includes viewpoint and opinion, narratives of memory that engage the minds of the learner are an important endeavor to undertake. Research supports this notion and emphasizes that lived experiences in students' lives are important (Delpit, 1998; Dewey, 1938) because very often these experiences determine and shape the way a student learns, perceives, processes and understands the material they are learning from a cognitive perspective. As college educators it is critical that we acknowledge the lives and experiences of our students if we are to enact change within them and allow for growth and new learning.

Educator Lisa Delpit highlights the concept of "culturally responsive teaching" and her research supports the idea that students need to see a connection between learning and their lived experiences. Linking that same notion to the respect needed in college classrooms for the lived experiences of students as culturally aware participants in a shared learning environment, Pink (2006) offers in his cognitive considerations the importance of the "narrative story" to pursue meaning and shares "when so much knowledge work can be reduced to rules and farmed out to fast computers and smart L-directed thinkers abroad, the more elusive abilities embodied by story narratives become more valuable" (Pink, 2006, p. 105). Pink (2006) provides ample examples of successful people who have delved into the essence of the stories embodied within their organizations to propel those institutions forward, to truly impact and effect progress, a very people endeavor that Pink (2006) finds paramount to recognizing the cognitive strength of the human experience.

Likewise, well known for his "funds of knowledge" theory, educational researcher Luis Moll posits that funds refer to the skills and knowledge attained by individuals through cultural and historical interactions. Honoring prior knowledge of students through life endeavors in the college classroom, these funds of knowledge can be utilized "to validate students' identities as knowledgeable individuals who can use such knowledge as a foundation for future learning" (Gonzales & Moll, 2002). Finally, Dewey (1938) regards education as the deepening and enriching of the quality of life, meanings, and significance. Dewey in 1938 stressed the unity of theory and practice as a "new" educational method emphasizing experience in academic learning, and contends that this "progressive education approach" must be rooted in the philosophy of human experience. Could this not still be true? What richer experiences can we harness in our students as college educators than the collective lived experiences we know reside within each and every student?

Some may speak of the "baggage" college students bring to the college classroom, but this is not baggage at all. Rather, it is a treasure trove that educators can help students mine as they process what they have experienced as lessons of learning. If we, college educators, approach the lived experiences of our students in this manner, we can then help them glean, mine, and apply these experiences buried within their cognitive capacities, as they embark upon the acquisition of new knowledge that will be stored permanently in their long-term memories ready to be retrieved in our varied and dynamic college classrooms, and their personal lives.

Various assessments of student learning, such as SUMA Information Systems and the ETS (Educational Testing Service), among others (2012-2016) have corroborated the effectiveness of the LEP teaching methods in increased student engagement and learning outcomes. Students taught through LEP designed courses gained a deeper understanding of concepts, extended their thinking to not only what concepts means but how they can be applied to life, and were able to recall the information when needed. Simply stated, utilizing lived experiences makes the topic under study more important for students because of the personal angle which makes it meaningful and serves as a more forceful memory retention tool. Elizabeth Barkley in her work on student engagement speaks of the importance of sense to meaning and the effects engagement can have on long-term memory. Barkley (2010) suggests that "information tied to survival or information that has a strong emotional component has a high likelihood of being stored" (Barkley, 2010, p.22) in long-term memory.

Information stored in long-term memory is ready to be retrieved and used to form new memories. Harnessing these long-term memories and utilizing LEP's inquisitive reflection to retrieve these memories to assist in new learning is the goal of LEP teaching methods. Long-term memories, through LEP, are tapped and enriched, broadened for the learner to inquisitively reflect, remember, and reuse so that the prior experiential events of their lives actually move forward to create new knowledge. By the use of LEP students become as Pink (2006) would like to see us consider "meaning makers." Both students and educators will benefit from the intrinsic reward of knowing they have made that difference all educators seek, while the data will show increased engagement and retention by students, increased learning outcomes, higher retention of students who feel connected to their learning, and increased graduation rates.

LEP is fully versatile and can be implemented across many disciplines. LEP is not a particular teaching method with specific steps to follow; rather, it is a concept of instructional design that allows teachers to facilitate learning in a personal manner in any discipline, and teaching and learning style. As educators plan lessons, regardless of their teaching style preference, the incorporation of LEP concept maps can be seamlessly inserted as per educators' choices to augment the disciplines' content.

LEP teaching methods speak to educators who face the challenges in engaging and retaining their students. But it also speaks to those same students who often face challenges in learning from instructors who do not consider varied learning styles. Since LEP teaching method links personal lived experiences to the course content students can more easily relate to a deeper interpretation of the material, and because of the contents unique application to themselves students can retain the newly learned material in the long-term. At a time when educational institutions of higher learning are concerned about student retention and degree attainment, and students bear the costs of this concern on many levels, why not consider an approach to college teaching that can help students see the value of what they are learning?

LEP teaching method has emerged as a successful and highly effective teaching tool because of its unique personal approach to hook the student's interest and the ability to make a unique personal connection to the material being learned. It sparks the students' curiosity as they explore and seek a memory, a personal connection, in which to frame, understand and interpret the new information using existing memories. While LEP is not an "end all" solution to challenges students and college educators face, it is a viable and successful option to increasing student engagement and retention by helping our students become engaged in our classrooms, in an environment where who they are and who they choose to be is valued as the stories of their life narratives and lived experiences are retrieved and utilized now and in future learning.

CHAPTER TWO

PRECOURSE PREPARATION

> FIRST IMPRESSIONS: SETTING THE TONE FOR LEP
> MIND SHIFT FROM CONTENT ABSORPTION TO CONTENT
> CONNECTION FOR MEMORY RETENTION
> LEP MIND MAPPING AND THE ROLE OF THE EDUCATOR

"I've come to a frightening conclusion that I am the decisive element in the classroom."

—Haim G. Ginott

Introducing LEP in the classroom is a fresh approach that is not only needed but quite necessary in order to increase student engagement and learning outcomes. However, it will require a steep learning curve for all college educators, and they need to understand that there are complexities involved; however, the benefits to students' and educators' own growth combined with vastly increased student engagement and learning outcomes quickly outweigh any challenges. LEP teaching methods are appealing to students because they meet the students' intellectual and emotional needs. Intellectually students are learning more and can retain the information because of the personal connections to content, and emotionally they are satisfied that they are learning and can apply that knowledge.

For students to learn in an optimal way preparation by the educator is necessary. It is so important that the students "master and not be mastered by the facts" (Dewey, 1964, p. 197). Students must learn in a way that they are not overwhelmed; thus, preparation by the educator is necessary at both internal and external levels. At an external level the classroom tone and environment become important aspects in learning through the LEP teaching method. Educators must create an active and trusting learning setting that allows for self-discovery, growth and the understanding of how the role of LEP's inquisitive reflection through personal inquiry of their lived experience enhances and enriches their learning. Students need a supportive environment to feel "safe" in order to share personal reflections.

At an internal level, educators must have the motivation to teach concepts and help students understand that learning through LEP requires a mind shift. In most classes learning is slated more to the present and the future, as opposed to the past. Students learning in this orientation do not look back; rather they look forward to find information. In these scenarios educators and students abandon past lived experiences and move forward without reflecting on the seemingly independent and unrelated experiences of the past that are such valuable opportunities for future learning.

As an educator, the teacher is the strongest influence in the classroom. Educators should organize the instruction in such a way that LEP not only assists in the learning and the memory retention of the material, but encourages insight and fosters growth (see Activity 4 preparation checklist). As facilitators of the LEP teaching methods, educators must exemplify the habit of using LEP's inquisitive reflection to address the concepts under study, and this must be done from the first day of class, as first impressions are crucial.

FIRST IMPRESSIONS: SETTING THE TONE FOR LEP

> *"My belief is you have one chance to make a first impression."*
>
> —Kevin McCarthy

First impressions are lasting impressions that often set the tone for the entire semester. The educator armed with an arsenal of tools and resources confidently walks into the classroom ready for the first day of class. The first day of class, no matter how many courses one has taught, is not an ordinary day of class for either the educator or the student. It is loaded with first impressions.

Think about the beginning of the term, the first day in a traditional classroom. Students file in, filling up the back, with the few eager participants in the very front seats. The educator greets the students and the class begins with a review of the syllabus. Not a bad place to start as the syllabus, the course contract, is very important, but how about mind-shifting a bit and beginning with a short personal get-to-know you session?

Never again will that educator have the opportunity of the first impression. Why not start off: if a teacher is to embrace the college classes from a lived experiences perspective, with a more personal message, an invitation, an acknowledgment of who the students are, where they are from, and what their goals are? College students need to know educators care about them beyond the course contract; this in itself is a motivator for a student to attend class. A "different" beginning, a fresh personal approach that lasts throughout the duration of the semester can make a significant difference in increasing student engagement and in-class retention. Some educators already incorporate this short interpersonal exchange in the first day of class, but why not invest greater energy and place a true emphasis on the importance of lived experience as a resource in understanding and remembering the content under study? Doing so will assist in the "buy-in" that this course is valuable to the student, and will increase engagement and retention rates.

Long-term student retention starts with the first day of class. First impressions have a major impact on college students' attitudes and can greatly impact the tone, course outcomes, and student retention for the rest of the semester. Thus it is very important for educators to introduce LEP practices if not on the first day of class, then shortly thereafter. By introducing LEP early, the educator will frame the class experience.

Information gathering about the class participants prior to the start of the course is recommended so that educators understand the class demographics. The educator, who chooses to implement LEP teaching methods within their own teaching style, must also be cognizant that the dynamics of the classroom cannot totally be predicted by this data. But knowing at least some information about students before class can affect how the course is designed and it offers an opportunity to modify and include more specificity in how lived experiences are sought and shared within that particular classroom. For example, if an educator knew that all of his/her students in a course were within a certain age range, say high school seniors enrolled in dual enrollment courses, LEP could be approached with a lens that would address seemingly common experiences that the educator may surmise that all of the students would be familiar with to augment the lesson plans.

Every educator should be aware of how the material being taught relates to the students' lives. The material must be relevant and clear for student engagement, so having a general idea of who the class participants are, especially when designing activities and assessments for later use that utilize LEP, can be very helpful for the educator seeking to encourage class engagement and increased course and learning outcomes. However, when expecting student buy-in, educators must be prepared to share their own personal experiences.

A few suggestions for how to handle the first day of a college class from the LEP teaching method perspective include:

> **Your Story**: Start by telling your story. It has been my experience as an educator for many years that when I begin telling a story and relate it to the concepts I am teaching, the attention in the class increases. Stories have a profound effect on students and memory, so why not engage them on a personal level and allow them to get to know you. This bond will assist in class retention later. So share and let the LEP teacher and student relationship flourish and watch as the classroom environment begins to transform from one of "when is this class over" to "I can't believe this class is already over."

The information shared does not have to be very personal; basic facts are just as interesting and engaging. It is important that students relate to their educators as more than just authority figures or subject matter experts, but people who have experiences that they remember and learn from, just like themselves. Start with basic information such as "Did you always want to be a college professor? Did you attend a similar college or institution? Did you have a challenging path to finishing your degree? Did life take you down a few varied turns before you landed here, at this, your current college? Do you have children, a dog or fish? What are you working on? What are your own goals? Why are you teaching this class?

It may seem awkward at first to share personal details about who you are and your own "lived experiences" but if you seek later to ask your students to tap into their lived experiences, sharing yours, at the beginning of the course, and then as appropriate throughout the course can clearly demonstrate to your students that you do value these experiences and that they are a part of the learning journey we all aspire to as being life-long learners learners—as human beings. You may even want to have a Power Point of photos showing where you grew up, where you went to college, or of your pet. The first impression can be welcoming and warm in this manner, highlighting that teaching and learning are reciprocal fascinating processes and that the course can be a new exciting learning adventure not only for meeting course and learning outcomes, but for self-discovery and students' personal growth.

> **Their Stories:** To initiate the sharing of the student stories on the first day of class where time may be a factor, it is best to keep things short and structured. The educator may initiate discovery by asking the students to introduce themselves and pick one thing about their life as it relates to why they are taking the course to share in class. Another approach is for the instructor to ask students to turn to another student in class and share this information for a smaller setting approach through a short discussion format. This is a fun exercise that will create bonds of friendships at the beginning of the course and socialization that may assist with finding a study partner and a friendlier environment for the student—which will assist in student retention.

Although these activities are designed to get to know students personally and rely on lived experiences, the information sought should not be "personal," and as such should not include any questions that would make a student uncomfortable. The questions should come from the content connection perspective as it relates to their life. For example, "Do you see any parallels to the course you are taking and your life? How do you think you will use this knowledge?" Students who share answers to these questions can reflect upon their own lived experiences in this subject, and in this way the educator can glean important information about his/her students as students self-report on their past lived experiences and prior learning.

Another approach to keep things very general and quick is to ask students to take a moment and write down answers to the question of: "How do I best learn?" so that they can be introduced to sharing information about themselves. The educator can highlight the various choices by students and talk about how learning from lived experiences will take place in class, a great segue way into discussing that important syllabus!

MIND SHIFT FROM CONTENT ABSORPTION TO CONTENT CONNECTION FOR MEMORY RETENTION

"There is nothing more powerful than a changed mind."

—Bishop TD Jakes

Reflective LEP teaching does not just happen automatically. A mind shift from "content absorption" to "content connection" must occur in both the educator and the student. In this paradigm the role of the educator is more of a facilitator rather than a transmitter of information. Reflective teaching arises as educators actively build and transform their pedagogical knowledge (Yost et al. 2000). To assist in the problem of student engagement and retention, new pedagogy must be formed that changes the relationship between the teacher and the students in learning strategies, and how learning is assessed (Dole et al. 2016). Fullan and Langworthy (2013) assert that unless a new pedagogy manifests students will become increasingly bored and unmotivated, and instructors will become frustrated and stressed. High stakes in the form of student learning outcomes and in-school retention is involved. Restricting pedagogy to traditional roots without the continuous exploration of fresh approaches that assists in learning and growth processes is a disservice to the students. Educators who want to see growth in student learning and engagement must find ways other ways to supplement their teaching. Failure to keep the students engaged and in the courses will have detrimental effects on student success and the college's financial state and future growth.

Whether you are teaching for the very first time or are a seasoned educator, preparing carefully for each course taught is mandatory. Precourse preparation on the part of the college educator embarking upon instruction using LEP in his or her college classroom requires a shift of thinking. The college educator who embraces the concept of LEP teaching methods needs to move from the mindset of "I have this information to impart upon these students" to "the students bring to class a wealth of life experiences upon which I can draw from to connect them to new learning, thereby creating the opportunity for a transformative process of meaning for each of them as they go through the course, learn, remember and enjoy the experience enough to move forward in their academic career." This is a monumental mind shift, but educators, like students, have within themselves the ability to mind shift, to move from traditionally held views of avenues of learning to a more dynamic outlook on what the college classroom can offer and the best way to utilize this living resource.

LEP is a progressive teaching style that embraces the mind shift from "content absorption" to "content connection" where new mind shifts will create formative results in students such as increased critical/reflective thinking skills, increased application of concepts through purposeful meaning and increased long-term memory retention of studied concepts, all which lead to increased learning outcomes and increased degree completion rates. By shifting the mindset from "content absorption" to "content connection" new information is easier to remember and recall because it is reinforced through the meaning and interpretation of the concept learned in a very personal way. Content absorption or memorizing information may assist in remembering the information learned for the short term, but content connection frames the information for understanding and cements it in the mind of the students through expansion of prior memories for easy remembering and retrieval when needed.

Whenever a person speaks, sees, reads, listens to or observes anything, he or she experiences a lived experience. The mind absorbs this sensory data, stores it and has it available for retrieval for future use. The mind learns and the mind remembers. The mind is a miraculous warehouse and the typical college classroom does not tap into the depths of dimensions that are possible through understanding and remembering information through personal meaning. Pink (2006, p. 13) shares that while the brain is complex, consisting of 100 billion cells or so, the actual "topography is simple and symmetrical" and that there is a current way of thinking that the left side of the brain, noted for reason and analysis, is not the dominant, but rather the equal partner to the right side of the brain which allows humans to recognize patterns, and interpret emotions, among other sensory abilities forethought to be of lesser importance. Pink (2006, p. 19) speaks of the powers of the unity of the two halves of the brain in terms of the mind in comparison to computers and offers a compelling case when he shares that "even the most powerful computers in the world can't recognize a face anywhere close to the speed and accuracy of my toddler son." What is even more fascinating, though, and linked to the use of LEP, is that the right part of our brains is activated in this exercise by recognizing the picture, but that the left side of our brain provides the thousand words that pictures speak, an adage that we all know and liken to the human element of not vision, but of seeing, of truly seeing something.

Through the use of LEP, educators are asking students to not only absorb the information presented, but connect to the information through their memories for greater comprehension. Students are asked to summon memories of lived experiences and lessons they have derived through their lived experiences, and to apply those elements to the concepts they are learning in their college classrooms. One could surmise that even Pink would agree this is a powerful use of the extraordinary minds of our students. Thus, one's lived experiences, filled with Pink's recognized senses, (two important ones noted here as story and meaning), form deeply rooted memories within students that can be harnessed for continued growth that flows from the lived experience and connects to concepts within the college environment. The idea is powerful when one really considers it and the implications for college classroom are enormous, particularly in improved learning outcomes through better memory retention achieved through LEP's personal connection to the content.

Research indicates that LEP personal reflection in studying new content completes the learning connection. Thus, educators must be able to shift to this recognition, to think about how what he or she is teaching can be embraced from this backward to forward moving lens, and focus on how they can assist students to mind shift as well. Students are asked to learn new material and study new concepts. But they are also asked to go back into their own minds to lived experiences only they can know, to make this leap and use this living resource as a memory retention tool.

The educator as guide and facilitator, along with being the course discipline expert, needs to think about how the minds of his or her students can be opened in this way. As students are shown how to delve into new information, new concepts, activating and connecting content to memory is paramount. Thus, asking the questions "what are the class demographics?" "How do I bring the lives and experiences of my students into the classroom and connect them to the content being learned, and keep them on point once they get there?" "How do I frame the concept for optimal understanding by the students?" "What format should I use to deliver each lesson for optimal results—class discussion, written assignment, lecture, group work or a combination of these?" become vital for the educator, and relevant learning takes on a much more important meaning.

LEP MIND MAPPING AND THE ROLE OF THE EDUCATOR

"Normal linear note taking and writing will put you into a semi hypnotic trance, while mind mapping will greatly enhance your left and right brain cognitive skills."

—Tony Buzan

A mind map is a visual diagram that is utilized to organize information (Hopper, 2015). Mind mapping offers a natural way of thought progression. LEP content mind mapping is one of the most powerful tools educators have available to increase student engagement and long-term memory retention of learned content. Mind mapping is one of the best ways to capture ideas, thoughts and concepts because a large number of students are visual and understand concepts with greater ease visually, rather than in auditory lecture or other formats. Mind mapping is an effective learning tool to help students brainstorm any subject and think creatively because mind maps allow students to see the whole picture, and how different thoughts are linked together, which makes learning enjoyable and comprehension of content being learned much easier.

LEP mind mapping connects content being learned to meaningful memories stored in our brain that can be used in future learning. Mezirow (1990) contends that meaningful learning is guided by experience and interpretation of that experience, which is a process of revising the interpretation of an experience that leads to new ways of thinking, valuing, and acting, all which lead to greater focus and retention of the content being learned. LEP's inquisitive reflection is a form of meaningful learning that connects content under study and leads to long term memory retention that is easily reinforced through mind mapping.

LEP mind maps can visually harness the full range of the content under study. LEP mind mapping activities of content learned are crucial in the learning and memory retention process as students determine the structure and sequence of their knowledge construction (lived experience) and seek to tie it into material being learned. There are numerous mind mapping activities educators have to choose from when developing their courses. Educators may select from any of the LEP mind mapping content memory retention activities included in the book to incorporate in their lesson plan, modify the existing activities for their particular discipline or create and customize their own. Educators should also get their students into the practice of developing their own mind maps as the content is being taught. Mind maps can be created by students through various formats such as students working independently with content graphing and outlining various aspects for full understanding of a particular concept, through stories, group work, and reading, among others.

We, as human beings, all share common experiences; why not use these lived experiences as a valuable learning resource, as often the content we are trying to teach our students is meaningless unless we can relate it to personal importance, and they can see that relevance? When constructing an LEP mind map, students should be directed to begin with a central concept and expand outward to more in-depth subtopics that will surface. A good visual is to have students connect a subtopic through branches stemming from the central concept showing the relationship to the concept. Because mind maps promote the use of single key words instead of whole sentences, students are able to review key concepts at a glance. Students can detect hierarchies between individual pieces of information and attribute relevance and meaningful links to the concept. Additionally, the visual aspects of an LEP mind map, along with their personal lived experiences will reinforce the content in their long-term memory.

Mind mapping content that needs to be learned through stories, works particularly well with LEP because stories are an effective way to transmit information between human beings in a more understandable, and memory retentive manner. Students remember stories more readily than facts and are much more interested in what the professor is discussing if the information is imparted through a story. Bough (2015) contends that stories are key in linking different events together that might have been lost in memory over time. For centuries, stories have been and still are an effective teaching method because of their appeal to the larger population with various cognitive processing levels. Stories are a means to present topics and help to organize, memorize and learn from our daily lives (Bough, 2015). LEP story mind mapping of the journey of discovery relating to the content being learned is strongly encouraged in every classroom.

Mind mapping stories as it relates to content can be an indispensably useful tool for understanding and long-term retention of information because students can visually see the progression and/or overall image of the content under study. Bough (2015) calls stories the foundation of knowledge in which we build new memories to add to existing knowledge. Thus story mind maps can be continuously modified to incorporate new information to gain a clearer understanding of the whole concept. Bough (2015, p. 6) further contends that "our brains are wired for stories, and we do not easily remember what others have said unless it is in the form of story." Bough (2015, p. 6) further contends that "stories are communicated effectively because speakers are mapping the mind for others to follow! The more skillful educators are at describing these experiences, the more vivid the picture painted in the students' mind and the more they can relate to your story… the more students' relate to the story, the more they comprehend." The more common the experiences and perceptions educators use in building the story, the more "lights" the story turns on in the students' mind (Bough, 2015). Thus, the more proficient the educator is in describing lived experiences as they relate to the course content taught to students, the greater the chances students will be successful in creating their own story mind maps to make sense of the concepts under study. When students can relate to the story, the more they understand, the greater the likelihood that they will remember the information for future uses (Bough, 2015).

Mind mapping the content that needs to be learned through storytelling from the LEP perspective can also increase the bond between the teacher and student because of the personal aspects associated with LEP teaching. Educators are encouraged to harness their own storytelling power to use in their courses to reach more students, which will increase learning outcomes and provide a richer learning experience and increased student engagement in the classroom and long-term memory retention of the material being learned.

Group work is also highly effective within the LEP mind mapping paradigm. Mind mapping within a group setting allows students to break down the content into smaller more manageable parts and offers students the opportunity to "see" and "hear" and understand the content through several perceptual lenses. Often a peer may be able to explain a concept that connects in a better way or makes more sense to other students, than that of the teacher, thereby facilitating learning for all students in the group.

Group mind mapping should be simple. To create a simple group mind map, students should write the concept in the middle of the page and as ideas flow all students in the group can create branches stemming from the center concept until the mind map consists of the exploration of the content through many perceptual lenses, and ends with conclusive summary of understanding. Mind mapping within a group increases creative ideas through brainstorming, aids in improved communication skills, and adds value in a side benefit of learning important life lessons in relating to cooperation and teamwork. But, in order to gain these benefits, students must be active learners, and educators should monitor groups ensuring all participants connect to the new information.

Another form of mind mapping as utilized by the LEP teaching methods is through reading. Educators are fully aware that reading and taking traditional linear notes is not always the most effective format for learning and memory retention. The note taking process is monotonous and time consuming. In comparison with taking notes, LEP mind maps offer a more effective strategy to learn and retain information because mind maps structure students' thoughts and allow for a clearer overview and clarity of the content.

When students read they are internally retelling the story and listening to other people's stories as they mind map their ideas and thoughts as relating to the material being read (Bough, 2015). This means that through reading students can create mind maps of the information that uniquely relates to them and the content being learned. The exercise of reading and then writing down pertinent information as it relates to the concept and how it applies to the students' lived experience is in and of itself a reinforcement of memory because repetition is a form of learning, and the information is now personally associated with the student.

As facilitators of learning within the LEP paradigm, the teacher is not the king or queen who controls all learning. The LEP educator is the leader who grants the learner space, creativity, and time for exploration, to not only understand the content under study, but offer an opportunity to learn of its application in the student's life. It is through embracing these responsibilities and extending learning by utilizing LEP mind maps that long-term memory of the concepts will increase.

When presenting material that will be transformed to mind maps LEP educators always need to think one step beyond the content of the discipline and ask. "How can I link this concept to the lived experiences of my students so that they can easily mind map the new learning? How can I help them make that connection for themselves and enrich the work they do in my class through mind mapping the content to enhance learning?" While course design is a professional exercise undertaken by the educator, infusing LEP is not always an easy route to visualize. However, in time as LEP is included in the college classroom and students share their lived experiences, the educator will see how readily the students are able to make the connections between concepts and their memories and improve their learning outcomes and long term memory retention. Teaching in this way, from a backward to forward lens valuing and embracing students' lived experiences and tying these indispensable memories stored in their mind warehouses to the course content for increased understanding and long-term memory retention is the essence of LEP teaching methods. It is a rich and worthwhile approach to learning that assists students to grasp concepts in a new way through mind maps, lived experiences and memories for genuine connection to the subject matter under study while enjoying the learning process.

Plan early and well. Being organized and well structured in your planning will greatly assist in deriving the most benefits gained through the use of the LEP teaching methods. Infusing LEP in the college classroom sets the stage for a myriad of possible highly effective approaches in how students are asked to react, learn and remember the material presented. It is an important mind shift from content absorption to content connection that happens through the vehicle of LEP's inquisitive reflection resulting in long-term memory retention.

Embrace the mind shift and be willing to change and learn. Be open to everything the LEP teaching methods have to offer. The mind shift in thinking necessitates pre-course thought and planning by the educator for increased student learning and course outcomes, as is done with every course, but the LEP teaching method has a unique feature which allows for optimal learning and memory retention, the lived experience, which will require additional preparation time.

The LEP teaching method is also a gift to education as a whole, as it offers something much more personal, inspiring, and enduring. It allows for the educators to be mentally stimulated in a fresh way, to do or feel something different, to be inspired and awaken to something new, which results in a fresh zest for teaching as their profession, and a more creative way to teach the material students need to know and remember. LEP teaching methods truly are a win-win for all.

CHAPTER THREE

TIME FOR ACTION

> LEP MINDFUL ENGAGEMENT
> INFUSING LEP IN THE COLLEGE CLASSROOM
> THROUGH MEMORY SYSTEMS
> + WORKING WITH MEMORY
> + LEP AND SHORT TERM MEMORY
> + LEP AND LONG TERM MEMORY
>   − LEP AND EXPLICIT MEMORIES
>   − LEP AND IMPLICIT MEMORIES
>   − PROCEDURAL MEMORIES
> + PRIMING AND CONDITIONING
> + TRIGGERS AND MEMORY RETRIEVAL

"Memory is the mother of all wisdom."

—Aeschylus

LEP MINDFUL ENGAGEMENT

Individuals do not automatically learn from their lived experiences (Ashford & DeRue 2012). Ashford and DeRue (2012) contend that two people going through the exact same experience may learn different amounts or fundamentally different lessons because of how mindfully engaged they were at the time of the learning. They further stress that to maximize the value of any experience, human beings must approach and go through their experiences mindfully and reflect on these experiences in ways that enhance the lessons of experience. According to Ashford and DeRue (2012), mindful engagement is a powerful mental process of how individuals can approach learning through their experiences with a focus on the learning orientation and greater learning from those experiences rather than focusing or judging experiences as failures, or past mistakes. Ashford and DeRue (2012, p. 149) contend that "mindfulness is a state of being where people are actively aware of themselves and their surroundings, open to new information, and willing and able to process their experience from multiple perspectives." Mindfulness within the LEP teaching methods paradigm also views mindful engagement in the same light and is focused on learning orientations which allow students to attain new knowledge or a deeper understanding of a concept through the memories of their past experiences.

LEP methods teach with the notion that experiences not only teach but are the best kind of educators because they are personal. The LEP model of mindful engagement create formative results through increased critical thinking skills and inquisitive reflection to enrich understanding and applications of concepts being learned through purposeful personal meaning, meaning that is created through the students' unique lived experiences. Mindful engagement in LEP increases student engagement and retention as a direct result of "mindful engagement" in the course content by the student because it forces them to actively and mindfully stay engaged in the learning process. This leads to increased long-term memory retention of studied concepts because students understand the material through a personal lens, and retain that information long term.

INFUSING LEP IN THE COLLEGE CLASSROOM THROUGH MEMORY SYSTEMS

> *"You are told a lot about education, but some beautiful sacred memory, preserved since childhood, is perhaps the best education of all. If a man carries many such memories into life with him, he is saved for the rest of his days."*
>
> —Fyodor Dostoevsky

Memories matter. Past memories matter. New memories matter. Memory is fascinating and holds a seemingly endless supply of information human beings can access when desired, but memory retention is diminished by lower memory ability, or motivation to remember. In a study on "Google Effects on Memory" researchers found that college students remembered less information when they knew they would have access to it later. "The internet has become a primary form of external or transactive memory, where information is stored collectively outside ourselves" (Sparrow, Liu, & Wegner, 2011) meaning people don't remember as much as they could because they know they can use sources "outside of themselves" such as Google to find the information if they need it later, which will achieve the goal in finding the information, but most likely will not achieve the goal of long-term memory retention.

LEP teaching methods do not rely on outside sources such as the internet as the information highway to assist in understanding and learning of new information. Instead, they look inward for personal memories and reflections to assist in the learning and memory retention process. LEP teaching methods ask that students look within themselves and search their memories for a framework in which to understand the information. Students enjoy learning through LEP because LEP peaks their curiosity as they explore and seek a memory, a personal connection, in which to frame, understand and assimilate the new information. It is an engaging tool for students to use to learn and remember information.

As students absorb the information through reading, lecture, discussion and so on, they easily move from content absorption or memorizing information, a method that most students rely on to get through assessments, to content connection which cements new information by providing a framework of which to understand and remember the information. Once the student gains understanding of the concept and assigns meaning to the material being learned using personal connections and significance, the new information will be stored in long-term memory with easier recall when needed. The material learned by personal connection is easier to recall later because it is reinforced through meaning and interpretation of the concept learned in a uniquely personal way.

Working with Memory

Memory is the best resource available for learning, but how does LEP work with the various human memory systems to achieve long-term memory retention of information? How does LEP shift the mindset of an individual from "content absorption" to "content connection" and activate the various memory processes, so that the end result is long-term memory retention and easy memory retrieval? To answer these questions LEP teaching methods employ three memory systems that are central to learning: sensory memory (senses related); short-term (working) memory where information is held while temporarily working with it, such as remembering a phone number just long enough to dial it; and long-term memory, which refers to the storage of information for an elongated time. Long-term memory is largely outside of the individual's awareness but can be summoned into working memory when needed. The three memory systems are very dependent on one another and play a pivotal role in learning.

Memory is essentially storing information for retrieval purposes. The strength and storage of the memory depends on the strength of the memory that the LEP involves; the stronger the memory, or the greater the importance of new information, the stronger the recall. Memory systems are intricate and complex in design, but in brief, the process of remembering information involves three steps: encoding (perceiving), storing (maintaining) and retrieval (accessing when needed). Since senses are linked to the central nervous system which is comprised of the spinal cord and brain, during every moment of an individual's life, sensory information is being taken in by sensory memory. Thus sensory memory is the starting point which creates a lived experience phenomenon (LEP) in which to learn and starts the process of memory retention.

LEP Memory Process

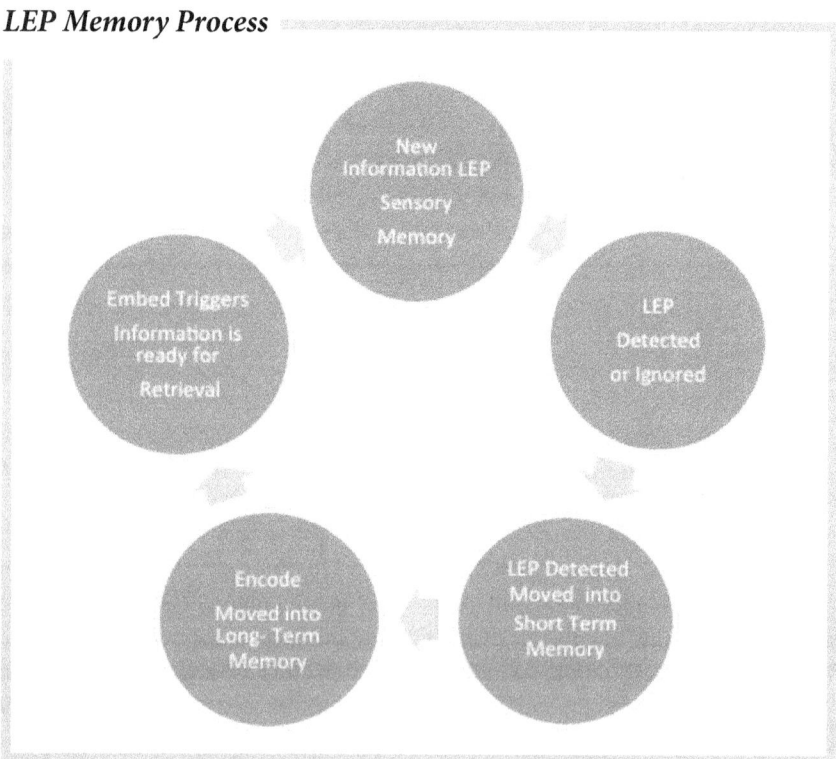

Sensory memory can be viewed as a buffer for stimuli generated by the five senses of sight, hearing, smell, taste, and touch. This perception or awareness often is out of cognitive control and is an automatic response that allows the individual freedom to either detect the stimuli or ignore it. If ignored, the stimulus immediately disappears from the mind. If detected, the stimulus is allowed entry into sensory memory and begins the LEP memory process. Even though this process does not require any conscious control, it does play an important role in storing information in short/working memory and eventually long-term memory.

Sensory memory is the first line of an imprint and allows for the information to make its way into the consciousness and temporarily rest in short-term/working memory. To reinforce sensory memory when teaching through LEP, external props should be employed. Props, such as pictures, images/visuals, colors, symbols and so on to assist in lecture, combined with the auditory effects of the educator, such as a raised tone of voice to emphasize important facts, associating information imparted with smell, using touch examples, or the use of mind mapping exercises specifically designed to capture sensory memories will aid in acquisition and encoding of the information into sensory memory. Moreover, reinforcing materials taught through sensory props or personal meaning will successfully move the information from sensory memory to the next step of memory processing which is short-term memory, which will allow students to work with this information until it is moved into long-term memory through encoding.

The LEP teaching methods utilize three main ways to encode information into memory, visual (images) acoustic, (sound) and semantic (meaning). Encoding is vital in the LEP process because it is responsible for creating a new memory (see Activity 5). Through sensory information and/or meaningful information encoding allows the perceived LEP to be converted to a construct that will be stored in the brain and available for later recall. The sensory input a person receives must be changed into a construct that the individual can understand so that it can be stored.

LEP Memory Model

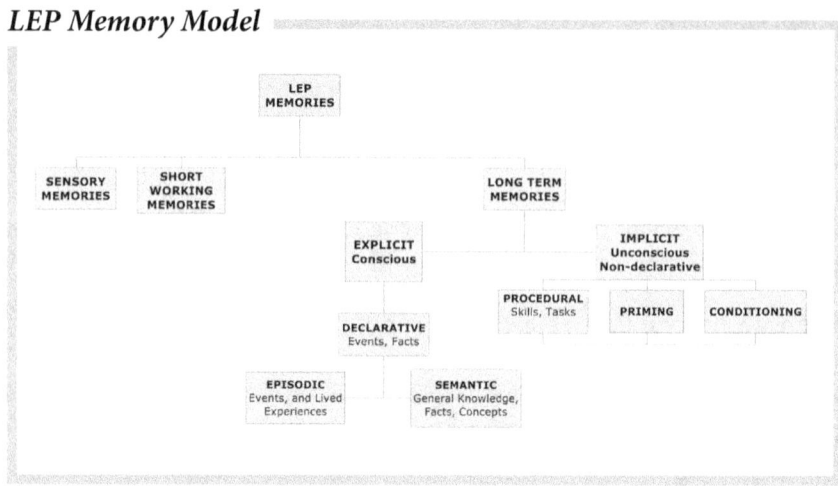

LEP and Short-Term Memory

New incoming information is easier to understand when it is framed. Framing concepts means that the educator will include a framework, a context of how the information is to be perceived before they impart the actual information. Experienced educators know how important framing is when introducing new information to students and often include a preview, an image, or some kind of a forward to frame the information they are about to impart, to better prepare the students for this information. When students hear the concepts later, they will now be able to use this frame of reference for better comprehension. Framing could be just a quick preview before the lecture allowing students to know what they will be learning, why they are learning it, and why it is important. Framing should not be optional, but essential, since it greatly assists in the comprehension and memory retention process.

Framing is a feature of our brain's structural design mechanisms. Human minds react to the context in which something is embedded and tries to find patterns or existing blue prints to create meaning. To frame a concept through LEP's inquisitive reflection students search their memories for an event or a situation that most closely resembles the concept definition under study (see Activity 6). Once a lived experience is identified, the students focus on the relationships between their current understanding of the concept and the main ideas and details of their lived experience. There is an unfolding of patterns and structures from exploration of the lived experiences as they are related to new concepts as the framing begins for better understanding, which is followed by meaning in the working memory.

Researchers describe short-term (working memory) as a memory system that has limited capacity and can hold and manipulative information for a short span of time. Short-term memory cannot be stored for later use, but it must be accessed immediately and used even as new information is surfacing that must be integrated. Short-term memory holds small amounts of information usually five to nine elements or less for short periods of time, typically no more than a minute before the information is either amalgamated into long-term memory (Miller, 1956) or forgotten. (Students should be encouraged to take the Memory Self-Test [see Activity 7] to test their memory skills).

Short-term memory can only hold a few chunks of new information briefly. The educator must seize this opportunity when presenting the information to students and assist them in the encoding process of moving incoming information from short term into long-term memory. Repetition of new information will assist in the encoding and prolong short-term memory retention, but personal examples either from the educator's life or the students themselves that connect to the content learned will significantly assist in the encoding of information from short-term to long-term memory. Time and attention are crucial in short term/working memory; the more attention and mental effort is placed on the stimuli in short term memory, the easier the encoding process into long-term memory will be. The stronger the embedded triggers, the easier it will be to recall the information.

Good LEP encoding techniques, when moving information from short-term memory to long-term memory, must include relating new concepts being learned (content absorption) to ones that the student is already familiar with (content connection) through LEP's inquisitive reflection. During the encoding process from sensory to short-term memory, the focus is to connect new information to the student's lived experience in a common way, so that it is practical, easily remembered and readily retrieved. If the students can connect information being learned with an event, fact, place, person, thing, feeling, situation, or any significant memory that exists within them, they can access that information later through a cue or a trigger when they need it.

If on the encoding journey through the memory systems the information does not illicit interest within the students, such as if the lecture or presentation is boring, or they feel detached from the material being taught, encoding has a very limited effect on learning. Students' engagement and interest in the material learned play a large role in the strength of the encoding process because even though parts of the brain such as Broca's area and Wernicke's area will be activated, the information mainly will be processed in the language part of the brain to decode the words into general meaning, without any real lasting memory in the student's mind. The lack of engagement means it is unlikely that the information will transfer from short to long-term memory, and most likely will be forgotten.

Information that has been transferred from short-term memory and stored in long-term memory can be retrieved through cues. Cues are vital because they serve as retrieval triggers that stimulate the brain to remember the sought information at a later time. Once the information is strongly encoded through a memory of the student's lived experience as relating to the concept under study and moved from short term/working memory to long-term memory, cues become extremely important. Thus during the encoding process from short-term to long-term memory, triggers must be identified and associated with the specific concept learned to initialize and cue memory recall of the concept later. Triggers can be values or things that are important to the students and can come in many forms such as smell, sound, pictures, touch, stories, events, dates, places, times, emotions, situations, opinions and so on. Some thought must be given to the appropriate trigger that will retrieve the information easily, as it is important to apply the most favorable stimuli to trigger memories relating to the content being learned for easier recall later.

LEP and Long-Term Memory

Schemas are an important component in the structure of long-term memory because schemas organize categories of information and the relationship among them. Students who are new to the topic have less well formed schemas in their long-term memory, thus it is harder to assimilate information. Students who have prior knowledge about the concept have more developed schemas absorb, assimilate and connect to the information quicker. The LEP teaching methods recognize this difference and adjust explanations of concepts accordingly; meaning that for those students who are new to the concept the review is generally taught at a slower pace, than when students have well developed schemas.

In moving information from short into long-term memory the LEP teaching methods plug into two key long-term memory systems, declarative/explicit and non-declarative/implicit. Declarative/explicit memory includes episodic and semantic memories that can be consciously recalled, and non-declarative/implicit memories are unconscious and include procedural memories, priming and conditioning. The greater the schemas of understanding and the larger the framework of existing information in memory systems, the easier it is to connect new information to it and remember it long term.

LEP and Explicit Memories (Episodic and Semantic)

The declarative/explicit memory system which houses episodic and semantic memories is of particular interest to the LEP teaching method paradigm. Explicit memories register the lived experience. The most significant form of explicit memory for subjective experience is the episodic memory (Solms & Turnbull, 2002) or autobiographic memory as indicated by Damasio (2010). Solms and Turnbull (2002) noted that this type of memory involves the integration of the two avenues of experience, the subjected state from the inner processes such as perceptions, coupled with externally sensed events through the sensory system, smell, sight and so on.

Solms and Turnbull (2002) further contend that the subjective experiences of an individual, itself initially unconscious and linked with memory traces of external situations, comprise the episodic memory and their lived experience. According to Solm and Turnbull (2002, p.161), "external events can be encoded consciously (as semantic, perceptual, or procedural traces), the episodic living of those events apparently cannot. Experiences are not mere traces of past stimuli. Experiences have to be lived. It is the reliving of an event as an "experience" ("I remember…") that necessarily renders it conscious."

Episodic memories include personally experienced lived events. Episodic memories record all lived experiences from which the individual can reconstruct the actual occurrences at any point in life. Episodic memories are the memories of autobiographical data that includes times, places, situations, events and involves the inclusion of personal meaning, interpretations, and emotions relating to the experience, as a part of the memory. Since many individuals make decisions based on how they feel, rather than what they know, episodic memories subconsciously play a strategic role in behavior and are an important part in new learning and retaining that material for future use. Deliberate strategies to employ episodic learning should be made by instructors as episodic memory techniques not only help students remember, but add to the enjoyment of learning (Sprenger, 1999).

Episodic memories are also driven by location. For example, if a person receives specific information, or bad news at a certain location, they will more easily remember it in the same location. Thus to reinforce this idea and help students remember the information being taught, educators should try teaching the various content from different parts of the room. Teaching from various points of the room will help students recall the information with greater ease during tests because they will link the location with the information taught (Sprenger, 1999) which should assist in easier recall.

Semantic memories are also important in the LEP paradigm. Semantic memories are everyday recollections, processed ideas and concepts that include a general knowledge of facts, such as knowing the functions of items or names of colors or that Washington DC is the capital of the United States. Knowing that a living

Christmas tree is green is an example of semantic memory; recalling what happened went you went to buy that green Christmas tree is an episodic memory.

LEP teaching methods use *the combination of episodic and semantic memories to reinforce new information* through LEP's inquisitive reflection. LEP's inquisitive reflection is particularly effective when probing episodic and semantic memories because it engages students' brains as they connect concepts being learned to their personal experiences and narratives in their own life. This interactive student engagement increases the ability to encode the information with greater ease and embed these concepts and new learning associated with it into their long-term memory at its deepest level.

In LEP's inquisitive reflection the individual reflects/thinks about something using explicit cognitions and first-person self-reference. Reflective memory through the probing of LEP's inquisitive reflection leads to self-insight and self-growth with an opportunity to expand the student knowledge with easier comprehension of the information being taught, because it is always easier to understand something when it can be linked to existing memories. For example, memories of people's faces, music that was playing, the smell of a Christmas tree might all be a part of a memory of an evening with family, but independently just the smell of the tree or a particular song that might have been playing that night will bring back that memory. Thus once new information is connected to an existing memory, the new information will be easier to recall. A strong LEP connection to new information being learned will reframe the content into a more personal connection resulting in a deeper understanding and an easier retrieval of stored information.

LEP and Implicit Memories

Implicit memory is a type of long-term human memory. Implicit memories hold implicit learning of any motor skill or cognitive activity. Implicit memories that are unconscious include procedural memories, priming and conditioning.

Procedural Memories

Procedural memories usually involve unconscious procedures and include knowledge of our motor skills such as knowing how to do things, like riding a bike or tying a shoe. Procedures or processes that are frequently repeated are stored in the cerebellum for easy access, and are used frequently in people's lives without their conscious effort. For example, playing a piano is dependent upon procedural memories. Many musicians and athletes credit their superlative ability to create procedural memories.

LEP teaching methods tap into procedural memories by connecting information that needs to be learned to procedural information that is already stored in the student's brain. There are various ways and hands-on techniques that can be used in conjunction with LEP in many subject areas to help students access procedural memory routes to learn and retain new information. Procedural memories are an effective learning tool in many disciplines, as problems that need to be solved may change such as in math or science, but the procedure or process to solve them often does not and follows a formal logical pattern.

Priming and Conditioning

Priming and conditioning are integral in LEP learning. Conditioning (associations) and priming (better and quicker response to a target memory based on previous exposure to related information) are both involved in learning, but the way they affect learning differs. As with procedural memories, priming also stems from the unconscious and influences people's LEP, yet individuals are typically not aware of it. Priming is the introduction of new information before the lesson begins in a way that students will recognize the information later. Priming is an interesting psychological phenomenon and often involves an unconscious memory of a past experience that reframes a perception of a current understanding which brings new understanding and faster recollection of the memory in the future. For example, if during priming, an individual sees the word "green," he or she will be slightly faster to recognize the word "grass" as the lesson progresses. If a student had just seen a movie on historic buildings, he or she is much more likely to notice related stimuli, such as historic buildings, on the way home from class. If a woman has learned that she is pregnant, she may start seeing babies everywhere. Seeing babies everywhere is the response to the priming of the recent lived experience of finding out about the pregnancy. Thus priming is the mechanism that activates representations and knowledge structures of an experience that influences the response with increased reaction time to the later stimulus. Priming also includes emotional memory, such as having intense feelings about things even when one cannot remember the situation or why they feel like they do.

In learning, when introducing new concepts, a student's brain tunes in to what is being taught. Thus promoting priming in the classroom in sensory, subliminal or through lived experiences, yours or their own, yields quicker understanding and better memory retention of new material, even if the person does not realize it. Individuals make decisions based on their subconscious input without ever knowing why. For example, in a study of memory priming North et al. (1999) discovered that on days that French music was played in a liquor store, more French wine was sold. On the days that German music was played, German wine outsold French wines leading the authors to suggest that priming has a significant subconscious effect on buyer behavior of customers, even though the customers were not consciously aware of why they made the choices that they did.

The same principle can be applied in the classroom when introducing new information. The students don't feel it happening, but the educators know and are actively engaging the student's brain. Helping students prime their brains for learning through any stimulus appropriate to the material being taught, even in very brief ways, before delving into the content can be of great benefit to the students' learning process. Thus, it only makes sense to prime students for the lesson at hand at every meet. Examples of priming can include various thoughts expressed to students on the subject matter, subliminal and stimulating messages, any type of sensory motivators, such as reviewing a worksheet or showing a class a related image or two of the content that is being introduced. Sharing your own personal connection (lived experience) to the material about to be presented also gives students an opportunity to connect their own lived experiences in their understanding of the material.

To prime the student's mind for new content in an optimal manner, the educators must always consider the subject matter and the priming delivery format to ensure the best content memory priming results, thus asking the questions "How is the student's mind to absorb this new information? What is the best priming delivery approach? Will priming occur through an image, sound, lived personal experience and so on?" If the senses perceive it, the mind processes it; thus priming presents educators with enormous opportunities for priming their students' brains for the specific content that will be presented in class and thereby setting the stage for increased understanding, engagement, and learning, along with increased long-term memory retention.

As with priming, learning through classical and operant conditioning is naturally aligned with the LEP teaching method. Classical conditioning is a psychological principle where an organism learns new behavior via the process of association, usually through repetition (Pavlov, 1897). It is a type of learning in which the stimulant acquires the capacity to cause a response that can be predicted because of repetitive associations. In essence, classical conditioning operates by linking two stimuli in order to generate a new response, meaning that it creates new associations between occurring events. For example, in some setting the words "say cheese" might be followed by a predictable camera flash and a smile on the part of the photographed person. The words "say cheese" (unconditioned stimuli) are associated with the camera (neutral stimuli) and produced a smile (conditioned stimuli). Thus classical conditioning (learning through association) can also be applied in the classroom by constructing two stimuli: new information (unconditioned stimuli) with a lived experience (neutral stimuli) that will produce new learning (conditioned stimuli). Additionally, classical conditioning can be used to enhance student engagement by creating a pleasant environment in which to learn. A consistent congenial learning setting will condition the student to enjoy being in class and at the very least alleviate some anxiety on the part of the student when sharing their lived experiences or when learning new information which should encourage attendance.

Operant conditioning learning is followed by reinforcement or consequence. The basic principle of operant conditioning is that behaviors that are followed by something pleasurable will be reinforced; the reinforcement will result in the behavior being repeated (Ormrod & Rice, 2003). Negative behavior will incur consequences. In the classroom operant conditioning is a way of learning through reinforcers, such as praise when a student performed well on a test or assignment which increases self esteem and encourages future performance. Thus praising students at appropriate times for their efforts is a primary reinforcer that will assist in a positive lived experience for the student. Positive lived experience assists in encouraging the student to continue the study efforts, which often leads to more study time, greater memory retention of the learned material, and easier retrieval. Consequences such as assigning additional homework should grades on a test be low are also effective in reinforcing the desired behavior, which is more study time, and better preparedness for the next test.

The LEP teaching methods draw on classical and operant conditioning as learning tools to increase learning outcomes because lived experiences influence the process of learning through conditioning. Lived experience is how individuals understand the meaning created through their embodied perception of something, or someone, often in an unconscious way. Thus, learning through conditioning can be a subliminal but powerful way to create meaning. The LEP teaching methods extend the classical and operant conditioning model by including the lived experience of the student's conditioned response as a tool for new reinforced learning and an important trigger to retrieve learned information from memory. By building operant conditioning techniques into lesson plans and connecting the content through the use of LEP, it is possible to enhance learning through reinforcements and increase learning outcomes.

Connecting conditioning to lived experiences as it relates to the content under study often assists students to better understand the conditioning functions and why they do the things that they do, which in turn allows them to make better sense of the content and their world. The LEP conditioning activities included in this book (see Activity 8 and 9) allow students to experience the effects of classical and operant conditioning on learning in the moment, which will assist them to reflect on and understand what conditioning is and how they can utilize it to understand and remember new information that is presented in class. However, as with any LEP mind mapping tools, the educators must take demographics of the classroom into consideration before working with the activities and modify accordingly, as not every student can connect with the same stimuli in the same way. For example, not every culture (lived experience) has a yellow school bus; thus the association of "yellow" and "school bus" may not be quickly made. Thus modifications to each course will be necessary for best learning outcomes.

Triggers and Memory Retrieval

Triggers are cues that retrieve information that has been embedded through long-term memory by encoding. Triggers are central to memory retrieval as creating effective cues and triggers are integral for remembering stored information. The power of the trigger depends on the initial memory encoding, meaning how deeply the information and trigger to remember it were rooted at the time of exposure and how closely it resembles the situation or relationship to the concept under current study.

Triggers must be used during all encoding processes. It is important to note that depending on the interference, moods and motive of the student at the time of the absorption and connection to the new information, some information may be harder to retrieve than others. That is why being mentally present in the moment to strongly embed triggers is critical; otherwise the information and the cue to retrieve the information will be much harder to recall. Educators should remind students that with any embedded memory, retrieval may be triggered by any cues of the context, the setting, sensory information, or a temporal link like morning or special days like anniversaries or birthdays, traumatic events or any other deeply personal connection. The student should always choose the most meaningful trigger as relating to the concept to cue the memory.

The LEP teaching methods mobilize various memory triggers to remember information learned (see Activity 10). Triggers unleash a conditioned response which LEP teaching methods use to initially assist in all encoding of information into memory. Episodic memories of relationships, feelings, thoughts and behaviors, or sensory perceptions, and semantic memories, which focus on dates or holidays, or places, are particularly ideal triggers for cued recall. Strong emotional triggers are also highly effective and will bring back strong recollections.

CHAPTER FOUR

IT'S PERSONAL: INFUSING LEP INQUISITIVE REFLECTION TO LEARNING

> INFUSING LEP INQUISITIVE REFLECTION TO
> CRITICAL THINKING
> TRANSFORMING LEP INQUISITIVE REFLECTION TO
> AUTHENTIC LEARNING
> LEP ORAL INSTRUCTION, WRITING, AND JOURNALING
> + ORAL INSTRUCTION
> + LEP WRITING
> + JOURNALING

"Education is not the learning of facts, but the training of the mind to think."

—Albert Einstein

Reflection is vital to learning. "Follow effective action with quiet reflection. From the quiet reflection will come even more effective action" (Drucker, 2011). Reflection leads to a personal connection by proving relevancy of the content being taught to students' lives. But this kind of deep reflection happens too rarely in college because self-reflection is not on their radar screens. Ehrlich and Fu (2013) contend, and the LEP teaching methods stress, that students have the time, space and motivation to engage in reflection because it is so important in learning. Thus, it is the purpose of LEP teaching methods to jumpstart that deep reflection by connecting students' lived experience to concepts taught to assist in new learning and memory retention of the learned material and develop deep critical thinking skills. If content is presented only by relaying facts and not creating connectivity, students will not retain the sum of that information and consider the information to be irrelevant and not applicable to them. Therefore, it is critical that educators not just present facts, but introduce new material with the emphasis on students' lived experiences to connect the relevancy of the content to the students' lives.

INFUSING LEP INQUISITIVE REFLECTION TO CRITICAL THINKING

Reflection springs from the Latin word *reflectere*, meaning "to bend back," bending back the mind to reflect (Valli, 1997). Dewey (1933, p. 9) characterized reflective thought as the "active, persistent, and careful consideration of any belief or supposed form of knowledge in the light of the grounds that support it and the further conclusions to which it tends." Boud et al., (1985 p. 19) interpret reflection as an activity in which people, "recapture their experience, think about it, mull it over and evaluate it." Sawyer (2003, p.5) defines reflection with more importance than simply student learning: "reflection is so critical; there can be no higher growth for individuals or for society without it. Reflection is the very process of human evolution itself."

Thus many scholars are in agreement that reflection is vital to human learning, but what significance does reflection have as a learning tool for academic educators? Why use reflection of lived experiences to promote critical thinking skills? Why is it important to use LEP's inquisitive reflection to harness students' past memories and apply it to learning? Because LEP's inquisitive reflection makes learning new information relevant to the students, stretches their mind, and allows for an opportunity to use mindful engagement, not only to work with their memory systems to retrieve information to connect to, but to frame and understand the new learning much quicker. Moreover, LEP's inquisitive reflection assists the students to critically think and question the connection of the concept to the lived experience and determine if a concept is understood, through the chosen memory frame, or if it merits further inquiry. Any method that is effective in stretching student minds and assists them to channel their natural curiosity in learning in a productive way is a significant instructional tool for educators. When students investigate and explore information being presented through critical thinking they bring forth the curiosity to learn more.

LEP's inquisitive reflection reigns supreme in promoting critical thinking skills because it requires that as students reflect on their past experience, they also must discern. Is there a connection between the memories I am retrieving and the content I am learning now? If yes, what is it? If no, why did that memory pop in my head if it is seemingly irrelevant to the topic being learned? The process of reflection is so powerful because it includes students asking themselves additional questions about what they did, how they did it, what did they learn from doing it (Boud et al., 1994), and how they felt about it (Boud et al., 1985) in relation to content.

When LEP's inquisitive reflection is utilized students must use discernment, judgment, and perceptions to critically think through ideas, thoughts, concept interpretations and connections. Dewey (1933) indicates that reflective thoughts are a quality of a creative mind "reflection is not simply a sequence of ideas, but a consecutive ordering in such a way that each determines the next as its proper outcome, while each in turn leans back on its predecessors." For educators, in the academic sense, LEP's inquisitive reflection is an effective learning tool that offers an opportunity through which students can use their critical thinking skills to order the mind, easily connect new information to existing memories, and enjoy the learning process.

LEP's inquisitive reflection is aligned with Boud et al.'s (1994) interpretation that reflection is concerned with students consciously looking at and thinking about their experiences, actions, feelings and responses and then interpreting or analyzing them in order to learn from them. One of the great strengths of Boud et al., (1985) research is the inclusion of emotions in the reflective action paradigm. According to Boud et al., (1985) reflection should include returning to the experience (meaning recalling the memory of the experience), connecting to the memory with emotions through the use of feelings, and evaluating the experience, which includes re-examining the experience with newly attained knowledge. The use of feelings is emphasized in LEP teaching methods, as feelings tend to reinforce memory patterns. When students reflect on their lived experiences which often include emotions, they deeply consider something that they may not otherwise have given much thought to which now they can use for learning. Spotting the patterns and links in thought that emerge as a result of students' reflections as they try to understand the material can greatly assist them in improving their critical thinking skills.

LEP inquisitive reflection is developing more than a set of skills; it is an expression of the natural relationship that exists between memories, learning, emotions and language. The process of finding the words to express something or to understand something from a new perspective will often distill and crystallize for students when their lived experience is used in explaining new concepts, and they see it with fresh eyes. LEP inquisitive reflection opens students' minds to begin the process of critical thinking and actively enjoying learning and encourages the willingness to examine prior beliefs and assumptions as they relate to their lived experiences, all of which reinforce memory.

Albert Einstein contends that critical thinking is the awakening of the intellect to the study of itself. Scriven and Paul (1987, p. 1) posit that "critical thinking is the intellectually disciplined process of actively and skillfully conceptualizing, applying, analyzing, synthesizing, and/or evaluation gathered from observation, experience, reflection," thus it is highly important in learning. However, research indicates that there is a lack of successful teaching and learning of critical thinking skills, as several studies by Sonoma State University (2015, p. 1) concluded, and emphasized that "critical thinking is not presently being effectively taught at the high school, college and university level yet, it is possible to do so." Since research indicates that the possibility exists that critical thinking can be effectively taught, it is within the power of an LEP educator to impart the skills and techniques of LEP to assist students to learn how to develop and apply critical thinking skills through reflection in their learning. LEP's inquisitive reflection will awaken the student's intellect and skillfully take charge of the structures of their memories to critically think and connect the concepts being learned to arrive at an expanded or new understanding or meaning.

LEP teaching methods through LEP's inquisitive reflection make effective teaching of critical thinking skills truly possible. Critical thinking calls for a persistent effort to examine any belief or supposed form of knowledge in light of the evidence that supports it. This effort and recognition becomes enabled by LEP through inquisitive reflection. By students making the connection between their prior experiences and beliefs through deep LEP inquisitive reflection of the content, critical thinking skills become honed and authentic learning takes place awakening creativity and new understanding. Thus, as Einstein asserts, "it is the supreme art of the teacher to awaken joy in creative expression and knowledge," and LEP offers educators that opportunity.

TRANSFORMING LEP'S INQUISITIVE REFLECTION TO AUTHENTIC LEARNING

LEP transforms inquisitive reflection to authentic learning through making personal connections between content learned and stored memories. By employing LEP's inquisitive reflection to lived experiences students can develop and refine their own critical thinking skills and be authentically creative in their learning process. Authentic learning typically focuses on real-world problems and their solutions, using a variety of classroom exercises (Lombardi, 2007). LEP is a form of authentic learning because it also focuses on real-world lived experiences and offers a wide variety of hands-on activities for uniquely personal in-class learning.

Authentic learning commands a real-life environment and an instructional approach in which information taught is meaningful to students. An authentic learning environment is successfully established in a classroom that is being taught using LEP teaching methods, as educators can easily present the information students need to know in a way that can be associated with "real-life" meaningful applications in a safe manner. By tapping into students' lived experiences and presenting content as it applies to them in a real world sense, students make connections in their brains and bring learning into a relevant and authentically memorable and meaningful context. Showing relevance to real life and using examples from students' or the educators' lived experiences engages the students in the presented material and assists them in making the connection to content under study in a very personal, and uniquely authentic way.

Lombardi (2007) contends that in authentic learning initially *learners look for connections*. Within the LEP teaching method this signifies that when educators impart new information, they must expand the relevance of the new material to students' lived experience for them to authentically feel that this information is important to them. The more encouragement learners have to become invested in the material on a personal level, the more engaged the students will become and the easier it will be for them to assimilate new information to existing memories.

Second, *long-lived attachments come with practice* (Bahr & Rohner, 2004). Concepts need to be reframed repeatedly and regularly, deployed in new contexts, and linked with new settings, activities, and people (Bahr & Rohner, 2004). As students learn and connect with the memories of their lived experiences, the concepts they are learning will be absorbed into long-term memory and authentic learning has taken place.

Third, *new contexts need to be explored* (Bereiter & Scardamalia, 1985). Within LEP new concepts being learned are always part of a much larger "learning event" and are directly linked to the learners' memories of lived experiences. When new information is assimilated with existing information new learning, understanding and authentic habits of the mind are formed which can further be explored, investigated or expanded to include future information.

LEP ORAL INSTRUCTION, WRITING, AND JOURNALING

> *"Of all the life skills available to us, communication is perhaps the most empowering."*
>
> —Brett Morrison

Communication is of utmost importance to being understood, having our needs met as human beings and our very survival. Human beings are in constant state of communication, although they may not be aware of it. In the academic arena, being effective in communicating generally means that you will be successful, thus LEP teaching methods place great importance on communications skills and encourage various types of interactions in the classroom.

Oral Instruction

Oral skills in the classroom are so important that according to the Department of Communications at the University of Pittsburgh, (2007, p.1) a key component of a well-rounded education has included speaking instruction, "speaking was considered an art…in which experience is gained through practice." Wilczynski (2009 p. 4) posits that "there is nothing more powerful and effective in the hierarchy of human communication than face-to-face verbal communication." Students arrive to class with a wide range of experiences in oral communications already. But to ease some public speaking fears LEP educators should inform students that in their lived experiences they have been communicating orally from an early age through informal speaking and that they will be encouraged to increase their oral communication skills in the classroom. Students may often be uncomfortable with public speaking simply because they had not had much opportunity to do so, "throughout their lives, students may have had experiences when they have used oral communication skills, while others may not have been encouraged to do so" (Communications, University of Pittsburgh, 2007, p. 1).

Educators using the LEP teaching methods can employ oral course activities that will improve their students' oral skills which will assist them in sharing their lived experiences with other classmates and have the confidence to ask questions in class. Students can also use this opportunity to learn about the lived experiences of other students as it relates to the concepts learned, problem solve and communicate about their assignments, group work and so on. To encourage oral skills in a non-intimidating way, particularly at the beginning of the semester, the educator can pair up two students in a group and pose a question from the previous class (Communications, University of Pittsburgh, 2007), or select a concept and ask students to share a lived experience that may be connected to the concept within a selected small group. This is a setting which should not be viewed by the student as intimidating because of the one-on-one, or a very small group approach. In this way the LEP educators will condition the students to speak to each other and share their experiences with a greater comfort level.

Oral activity reinforces course content memories and allows students a discussion with each other that may bring forth information that they may not have recalled on their own. The content is then more firmly encoded into long-term memory, thereby increasing learning. Once the small group had a chance to orally discuss the concept, the discussion can then be opened to include the whole class. This activity provides increased student participation as students gain more knowledge of the subject under discussion from the understanding of the concept as seen through their classmates' eyes. Opening the discussion to the class is highly beneficial "such a strategy effectively restructures the social organization of the classroom, from an exclusive emphasis on students speaking just to the teacher, to students communicating with each other" (Communications, University of Pittsburgh, 2017 p. 2). Assigning a full presentation by each student to present independently in front of the class once a public speaking comfort level is achieved is also recommended to increase oral communication and public speaking skills.

Students should always be reassured, feel supported and encouraged when speaking in the classroom, especially when presenting information. Many students fear speaking in front of an audience. In fact, Wilczynski (2009) determined that fear of public speaking is a threat that ranks with death, and is most humans' number one fear. Wilczynski (2009) also added that a helpful technique to calm this fear and anxiety in students is to practice relaxation exercises, visualization techniques, and most importantly, place emphasis on knowledge and purpose of the topic about which they are speaking. Allowing students the time to practice sharing their lived experiences as it connects to the topic under class discussion will greatly assist them to overcome their fear of communicating in class. There are various activities that LEP educators can implement for students that will develop increased oral communication skills. Small group work, presentations, and interviews are just some ideas to provide an opportunity for students to develop the experience needed for successful speaking skills.

Interviews are another way to lead students to increase oral skills by sharing their reflections as it relates to the content learned. An educator can interview a student, or students can interview classmates as it relates to the knowledge of the content under study. It is advisable that the educator set aside time at the end of a learning sequence, lesson, or school day for students to question each other about what has been learned, what they understand, and what is still not clear. Interviews also provide educators and students with opportunity to model and practice a variety of habits: listening, thinking and communicating with clarity and prevision, questioning and so on. Interviews also provide an opportunity for students to share lived experiences and to acquire new connective memories from their classmates' personal perceptions, and can greatly assist in learning and memory retention.

LEP Writing

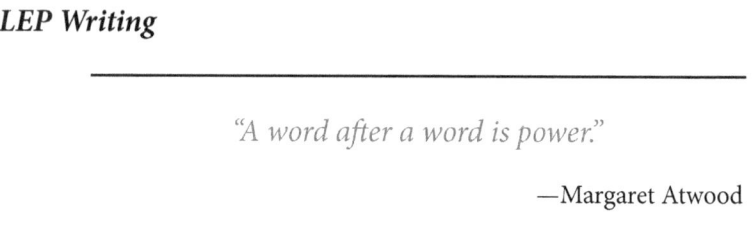

"A word after a word is power."

—Margaret Atwood

Between 3000 BC and 1000 BC writing was invented. Writing is so important to human civilization that Walshe, (1987, p.1) contends that "writing is humanity's second greatest invention…taking language from the invisible mind and make it visible on paper where I can work on it with full attention until it becomes the best thinking, the best learning, of which I am capable." Tom Standage asserts that "writing, which allows for travel across space and time has done the most for human progress."

Writing, to date, continues to be vital in learning and a sound fixture in academia. Writing, learning and reflection are closely related and can often dictate academic success. Students' academic success, according to Astin (1985), depends on students being able to effectively communicate and complete required assignments. Sentence and paragraph structures, punctuation, spelling, grammar, the ability to quote, paraphrase and summarize from various sources and just following a specific format are all very important aspects of writing, as without proper grammar and spelling, confusion and misinterpretation would reign. However, there is much more to writing than being structurally and grammatically correct. Writing is more than just relaying messages as it can elicit deep emotions that can in turn be used for new learning and memory retention.

LEP writing is that authentic writing that elicits not only deep emotions but is a master at expressing students' thoughts and understanding of new and existing information. LEP writing is writing students genuinely want to engage in. Educators often are challenged to develop activities in which students can write "authentic" pieces using real-world experiences. Not just research, but authentic writing, in which the students see themselves in the narratives. LEP writing is meaningful, purposeful and because it pertains to new information learned in a personal way relevant to the student. It extends past the requirement of the assignment and asks that students apply their lived experiences to connect to, reason, critically think, and explain the concept under study in written form which allows them time to contemplate the information and gives them a voice in their work.

If educators want students to learn to the best of their ability through writing assignments, the assignments must excite the students' interest. Written assignments are highly complementary to LEP teaching methods as writing is a task that invokes critical thinking skills, assists in the processing of course content, and promotes authentic and personal learning. But students will not give their best effort if the subject matter is not interesting to them. Students are much more motivated when there is a purpose behind the task, especially if that purpose is something that sparked their curiosity, and holds for them a personal gain.

It is not just theorizing research. LEP writing works with personal material, the students' memories of their lived experiences. The best LEP writing happens when the students have fully reviewed the content under study and now allow for LEP's inquisitive reflection to design its own course while it searches the students' memories for a point of reference to connect to, but without any imposed expectations, biases, predispositions or presuppositions. LEP writing is an organic life experience and sharing process in which critical thinking skills in combination with LEP's inquisitive reflection vastly increase student learning because they easily assimilate and process new information. Written assignments can range from brief reaction papers to a concept, completing LEP mind mapping worksheets, journaling, blogging, or a multiple page research paper. Other examples of written assignments include having students answer specific questions from the chapter or class lecture in written form, or write about a video shown in class using LEP as a tool of thought processing, reflection and comprehension. A student may also write a lengthy self reflection paper relating to key concepts in the textbook or lesson plan.

LEP writing takes a more personal approach to understanding and grants students a platform to learn and remember information in a way that is more effective than just reading the material in the textbook and taking notes. The LEP writing assignments provide students with an opportunity to ponder at great length, think deeply about the content as they write, and read and reread their entries to see if they truly understand the material. Giving students' ample opportunity to write in a course using LEP as a learning tool is a powerful way to engage students and increase their comprehension of the material they are learning. Expectations for written assignments must be clear, explained in detail and must include preparation for the LEP experience as well, as a grading rubric.

Some form of LEP writing should be required in every course. The main purpose of LEP writing exercises is to jumpstart the process of inquisitive reflection and examination of experiences in written form and connect these memories to information being learned. By encouraging introspection through LEP's inquisitive reflection and examination of experiences as they relate to the concept in written format, students utilize important writing skills that will lead to an easier process of "content absorption" to "content connection" within their mind.

Journaling

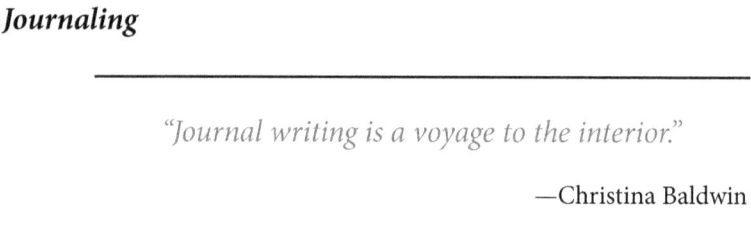

"Journal writing is a voyage to the interior."

—Christina Baldwin

Reflective journaling is widely used across all disciplines and has been found to be an effective learning tool. However, many students do not understand the benefits of journaling and see it as busy work. At the onset of the course it is important to assist students to reframe the mindset that journaling is more of a chore than a benefit. A journal should be perceived as a beneficial means that allows students to stop and spend time on their thoughts and informally put them into writing. Manjusvara (2005, p. 10) stated "the practice of writing takes us to the heart of ourselves. . . ." The practice of writing in journals allows students to think cognitively, contemplate and process the material under study, and interpret why that information is important to them in a very informal way. In journaling students are not answering questions, solving problems per se, but are using the journal as an informal information highway of their thoughts and understanding about the content they are studying. By modifying prior assumptions and perceiving the journal as a powerful tool to retain and review information in a very personal way, students will advance their own knowledge and strengthen their creative and writing abilities.

There are many benefits to using an LEP journal in the classroom. Journaling is an important element of LEP because of its critical thinking skills components and ability for students to privately see the world and concepts within it through a personal lens. Journaling also affords the students the ability to include feelings in their summation. Not only about what they are learning, but how do they feel about what they are learning. A journal very often is compared to a mirror because in life's various nuances it functions in the same way. According to Johns (2010, p. 28), "journaling is a mirror in which you can see yourself in relationship within the particular experience." Because the students are learning from a personal point of reference, students see themselves, find power in their voice and can freely write down ideas about the concept as seen and related to their lived experience. This type of journaling allows for writing without forced resolutions and will significantly increase creativity and assist in memory retention.

LEP journaling is reframing the lived experience to authentically connect to the subject matter to gain a clearer understanding and increase memory retention. The LEP journal can be used as a useful study guide for future tests, a practice tool for creative writing, or for personal reflections. Moreover, through the LEP journal activities, students will gain a full understanding of the concept's applicability in their life. Journaling is a process in which a personal understanding occurs as students synthesize content material as they practice writing about the connection between the content and their lived experiences.

Journaling can help with personal growth and development. Keeping a journal sharpens mental skill and creativity. In a study by Bruster and Petersen (2013) the authors note that students who wrote in journals wrote significantly more complex investigative reflections of classroom events over those who used weblog. Entries do not have to be long, but should contain the chapter number in which the concept is found, or the date of the lecture, and should reflect a clear understanding of the concept as it is connected personally to the student. Each entry should be dated, and the student should be reminded to use their journal after every class to write down thoughts about the material learned in class for that day and connect them to their lived experience in a continuous evolving text format to review and reinforce the information learned to memory. Journals may be reviewed by the educator at random; however, a short regularly scheduled review by educators will greatly assist the educator to assess if students are working in their journal and if that work is satisfactory.

It's Personal: LEP Problem Solving

LEP Problem Solving through Creative Visualization
Creating Transformative Meaning in Problem Solving through LEP's Inquisitive Reflection

> *"We are inclined to think of reflection as something quiet and personal. My argument here is that reflection is action oriented…the most eloquent and socially significant form of human action."*
>
> —Stephen Kemmis

Reflection is an active human action that is essential in order to problem solve. In all college-level disciplines, students are presented with problems to solve from mathematics to English composition to social sciences. There are strategies of problem solving that are applicable to resolving problems in any endeavor or any task. However, every field and situation calls for specific knowledge and specific habits of mind to apply to solving problems. LEP teaching strategies emphasize the applicability of these specific habits of mind that allow students to utilize inquisitive reflection of their past lived experiences to look for solutions that solve these problems.

LEP's inquisitive reflection is one of the most effective techniques to assist students to hone in their problem-solving abilities because it utilizes both analytical (logical) and creative (imagination) problem-solving abilities. Analytical and creative problem-solving abilities rely on different skill sets, but both can be used with LEP's inquisitive reflection to problem solve. Analytical thinking is logical, left brain thinking. Analytical thinking is beneficial in solving convergent problems because of its linear traits and step-by-step process to draw a conclusion. Convergent thinking is systematic, uses analysis, relies heavily on logic, and usually includes only one single solution to solve a problem. When students utilize convergent thinking, they are applying logical steps to determine what is the single best solution to solve the problem.

Creative thinking is right brain thinking. Divergent thinking aligns itself more with creativity and looks at many factors to find a solution from multiple avenues that are unique and would work to solve the problem. Divergent thinking allows for open-ended creativity in problem solving. Through divergent thinking and exploring memories of their lived experiences, students may discover solutions they did not know existed before or find numerous solutions to problems that may have equal value.

Both analytical and creative problem-solving techniques use critical thinking skills and their lived experiences to problem solve. Critical thinking skills of applying, analyzing, synthesizing and inquisitive reflection of lived experiences enable students to deal effectively with social, academic and practical problems from a personal perspective. Merely being presented with knowledge or information is not enough. Shakirova states (2007. p. 42) "for students to learn and practice problem solving skills they must be able to think critically."

Cherry (2016) denotes that problem solving is a mental process that involves discovering, analyzing and solving problems. This involves all of the steps in the problem process: discovery (awareness of the problem and the decision to tackle the issue), analyzing (understanding the problem, research, and available options) and problem solving (taking actions to achieve goals). Cherry (2016. p. 1) further notes that, "the ultimate goal of problem solving is to overcome obstacles and find a solution that best resolves the issue." But, often, it is a challenge for students to overcome obstacles in problem solving, thus, educators using LEP teaching methods must guide students to explore problem solving strategies through the use of their lived experiences as a point of reference.

But before students can be asked to solve problems through LEP, they must know how to recognize a problem, or understand the mechanics of a problem. Many students have difficulty in identifying the problem; thus the educator should model the problem identification process, or ask pertinent questions such as: what can you see that causes you to think there is a problem? What is happening, with who, where, how and why that you think there is a problem? The educator should assist by offering helpful suggestions, and guidance, but minimal assistance should be given allowing students to work through the problem identification process themselves until a discovery is made, and the students can perceptually recognize the problem.

Once a problem is identified, students are ready for LEP's deep inquisitive reflection of memories as it relates to solving the problem. By delving into past lived experiences students can begin the reflective inquiry of the problem solving process. George Polya, a famed mathematician, in his book *How to Solve It* (1957) identifies four basic principles of problem solving that is used by the LEP teaching methods. By introducing these principles in the classroom, educators using LEP teaching methods can impart the steps necessary for students to achieve problem solving techniques that will serve students throughout academia and in life.

The *First Principle: Understand the Problem* (Polya, 1957). According to Polya (1957), this principle can be implemented by assisting students to understand and clarify the problem to be solved. Students must identify the many facets of the problem before they can begin to look for a solution. To begin the problem solving activity, educators can pose questions to students to achieve a better identification and understanding of the concepts under study. For example, educators may ask pointed questions to achieve inquisitive reflection such as: Is there any facet of the problem that relates to your personal experience or a similar experience that you have heard about? What approach was used to solve it? Was the approach to solve the problem successful? Why or Why not?

Polya's (1957) *Second Principle: Devise a Plan*. LEP teaching methods are aligned with Polya's (1957) second principle and provide logical steps that students may want to use to devise a plan such as look for a pattern from reflection of past lived experiences, eliminate possibilities, and use direct reasoning. Patterns of reflection of lived experiences can be very telling and profound and highlight many unique ambiguities about a person, such as the same way they approach a problem. Eliminating possibilities offers students an opportunity to organize information, evaluate which information is important and which should be discarded, and removes possible answers until the correct answer remains.

Educators should assist students to devise a plan to solve a problem. Probing questions such as have you experienced this problem before? Or have you seen the same problem in a slightly different form in your life? Can you remember a related problem? Do you remember how you solved it? What worked? What did not work? These prodding questions force students to reflect and remember, and thereby form new critical thinking skills that allow them to connect to similar situations in their life and begin the process of creatively developing new solutions for the problem.

Polya's (1957) *Third Principle: Carry Out the Plan:* At this stage persistent and patience is needed. Students should continue to use LEP's inquisitive reflection to persist in finding solutions to the problem. It is important to remember that no single procedure or process works all the time—each problem is slightly different; thus, returning to inquisitive reflection for further problem-solving probing, as needed, is recommended.

Polya's (1957) *Fourth Principle: Look Back.* Polya (1957, p.4) mentioned that "much can be gained by taking the time to reflect and look back at what you have done, what worked, and what didn't." Asking questions such as, "How can I use this information in my life to problem solve in the future? How can I remember this information so that I can retrieve it later when needed?" is integral for students to predict what strategy to use to solve future problems. Moreover, utilizing the students' memories to problem solve will reinforce the memory of the problem solving experience to be used as a reference point and tool in another situation at a later date.

LEP PROBLEM SOLVING THROUGH CREATIVE VISUALIZATION

"Imagination is the only key to the future. Without it, none exists. With it all things are possible."

—Ida Tarbell

All human beings have the ability to mine their own unique skills to problem solve in their life. Ralph S. Marston, Jr. contends that "everyone has great potential based on his or her unique values, talents, abilities and possibilities for achievement." But these abilities have to be used and expanded in order to achieve greater skills particularly in problem solving techniques. Changing perspectives and looking at old paradigms with fresh eyes is necessary and can very often lead to new creative solutions, and increased motivation in students. According to Moses (1982) conventional methods around problem solving have centered on three general approaches: organizing instruction by content area; organizing instruction by strategy; and organizing instruction by presenting many varied problems. Moses (1982) further contends that each approach has demonstrated a degree of success in improving problem solving abilities of students.

LEP teaching methods do not deviate from the established approaches as noted by Moses (1982), but offer a supplement to the problem solving techniques in the use of creative visualization in reasoning and solving problems in academia. Creative visualization simply means that it uses creativity (imagination) to visualize the past and future probabilities. The use of creative visualization in learning is less popular in the mainstream of education, but can be just as effective as other tools such as analytical thinking to problem solve. Additionally, creative visualization can be a powerful way to sharpen memory.

Creative visualization's power comes from a mental technique which uses the students' imagination to generate and process visual mental imagery of the problem as an obstacle that is easy to side step, thus assisting them to move forward in visualizing the answer. Students who employ their imagination to generate imagery use their memory of lived experiences to create the images from the past to envision how the problem can be solved in current time and in the future. By combining creative visualization with LEP's inquisitive reflection students can become quite skilled at problem solving and learn from the experiences of their own life.

It is necessary to fully explain to students what creative visualization is and how to employ it in the problem-solving process. It is important to note that in order for students to begin creative visualization, they must have completed the identification of the problem. Once the problem is identified, students should be instructed to purposefully search their memories and use their imagination to creatively visualize ideas for solutions. Students should visualize every step in the problem solution process, and entertain various end results.

 The clearer the visualization of the problem, and the steps that must be taken, the clearer the answers and solutions to the problem will appear. When used correctly, creative visualization is an effective problem solving tool within the LEP paradigm because creative visualization can bring measurable changes in the way problem solving is seen and approached and offers a glimpse into the various end results. Creative visualization is a skill that all individuals have and should tap into to assist in the learning and problem solving process (see Activity 11).

Creative visualization through inquisitive inquiry becomes easier with practice, and is a technique in which students personally grow, increase their learning and memory outcomes, and enjoy. To get students started to begin the creative visualization process educators could pose a simple but practical problem. For example, an educator can ask students to solve a problem through creative visualization of getting to class on time tomorrow. What can the student imagine the steps should be? What can the student visualize about possible obstacles or events? What is the end result? Do they see themselves successfully sitting in class on time? Students should create a mental picture of the experience exactly as they want it to take place, meaning see themselves get up in the morning, and problem solve in their mind until they reach the point where they are sitting in class on time.

Practice makes perfect, and students should be encouraged to use creative visualization to solve their problems as much as possible. Students should be reminded that problems tend to be similar; they are just packaged differently. A change of an approach and the addition of creative visualization in problem solving will lead to seeing the problem in a different light and often the solution, instead of being impossible to find, will become obvious.

CREATING TRANSFORMATIVE MEANING THROUGH LEP'S INQUISITIVE REFLECTION

Integrating transformative meaning into learning and problem solving has many benefits. Transformative learning is based on the principle that personal experiences are an integral part of the learning process where a learner's interpretation of the experience creates meaning (Mezirow, 1996). Transformative learning offers a theory of learning in which meaning structures are understood and developed through reflection, and offer an explanation for change in meaning and orientation which holds that the way learners interpret and reinterpret their experience is vital to their understanding and problem solving skills.

Students being taught by the LEP teaching methods are introduced to various techniques that allow them to transform their lived experiences and reinterpret the experiences to make new meanings and connections and use that information to problem solve. Mezirow (1996, p. 196) contends that "learning is understood as the process of using a prior interpretation to construe a new or revised interpretation of the meaning of one's experience in order to guide future action." In a similar fashion, LEP teaching methods through inquisitive reflection transform textbook meaning to personal meaning and guide students to interpret and frame the new information in a much clearer and applicable way and use this experience to problem solve and guide future action.

Mezirow (1991) presented fours ways in which he sees transformative learning: by refining or elaborating our meaning schemes (existing points of reference); learning new meaning schemes (new frames of reference); transforming meaning schemes (habits of the mind); and transforming meaning perspectives (transforming point of view). Each of Mezirow's presented ways is aligned with the LEP teaching method, as it is with changing schemas within the students' lived experiences that new learning takes place, and the ability to problem solve increases. Moreover, Mezirow (1991, p. 167) added that for learners to change their meaning schemes "they must engage in critical reflection on their experiences, which in turn leads to a perspective transformation." Mezirow (1991, p. 11) further stated "because transformative learning is not about just acquiring knowledge but making sense of or giving coherence to our experiences; it is a meaning making activity" and "can greatly assist in problem solving."

In psychology, "meaning making" is how individuals understand, interpret, perceive and makes sense of their life, their relationships and the "self." A classroom using LEP teaching methods emphasizes the importance of this meaning making activity to connect to the memories of these lived experiences for transformative learning and to problem solve. Experience is seen as socially constructed thus; it can be deconstructed especially within the confines of the mind of students where any possibility can be explored vividly with great interest and engagement, and every problem can be solved in numerous ways. Students love learning about themselves and the world as it pertains to them. Students also love to tell their friends what they are learning, if it is invigorating. Thus why not give them that opportunity and introduce LEP as a learning tool? When students are connecting concepts with concrete applications they have connected to new meaning and expansion of their problem solving skills and general knowledge.

CHAPTER SIX

IT'S PERSONAL: KNOWLEDGE ACQUISITION THROUGH INFORMATION SEEKING

> LEP AND LEARNING STYLES
> INFUSING LEP THROUGH CONTENT, STORY,
> DISCUSSION, GROUP WORK, AND BLOGS
> + CONTENT
> + STORY
> + DISCUSSION
> + GROUP WORK
> + BLOGS

"The art of teaching is the art of assisting discovery."

—Mark Van Doren

Discovery and knowledge acquisition are extremely important in the information seeking process. But discovery and knowledge acquisition should be made by the students. The educator is only there to assist in the process. In this way the information is much more personal, relevant and better retained. Knowledge acquisition through information seeking within the LEP design considers an academic curriculum and strategies that are designed to provide opportunities for students to adopt a personal critical thinking approach to knowledge construction by using their memories to gain new insights and understanding, and draw upon students' personal values and ethics to connect to information being learned.

Information seeking is vital in human learning. According to Marchionini (1995, p.1), "information seeking is a fundamental human process in which individuals purposefully engage in order to gain knowledge, and is closely related to learning and problem solving. Human existence is characterized by the notion of search, seeking information and experiences, and this seeking connotes the process of acquiring knowledge." The process of acquiring and using information is a critical activity that becomes more fundamental and strategic with practice as students make genuine connections to new information using their lived experiences and continue to work using their reflections as frameworks to understand concepts.

LEP information seeking is a process of inquiry that results in knowledge acquisition. Information seeking through LEP assists students to develop analytical and inquisitive reflective skills in relation to information seeking, sources of information, and understanding new information. Often students need assistance to achieve this; thus to help students understand the complexity of the material under study, educators must engage them in effective LEP information seeking connections. Much of information seeking requires identifying and retrieving previously stored information as it relates to the subject matter being learned. Educators using the LEP teaching methods can design custom and specific learning exercises or create mind-mapping activities to assist students in information seeking endeavors.

LEP information seeking is a high-level cognitive process as it uses memories to acquire new knowledge. Knowledge acquisition through searching memories give students motivation to learn because students' emotive selves gain pleasure from seeking, and integrating new information as they are learning because that information is personal, relevant and meaningful to them. According to Pahomov (2014, p.1720), "meaningful reflection is the only way we grow as humans" and, "for student reflection to be meaningful it must be cognitive, applicable, and shared with others." Thus LEP information seeking in an academic setting is a powerful tool that can assist to navigate some of the barriers students face in information seeking.

LEP AND LEARNING STYLES

"Tell me and I forget. Teach me and I remember.
Involve me and I learn."

—Benjamin Franklin

Just as educators have a preference for teaching styles students have a preference in learning styles. Traditional learning is generally in the form of linguistic and logical book based teaching, with much repetition, and the use of various assessments to reinforce, review and grade the information. According to Shattuck (2016), all educators teaching a class want to be understood; however, when students are equipped to learn best in distinctly different ways, how the information is imparted by the educator is crucial. Educators need to know how to embrace various learning styles while imparting LEP basic principles so that all students benefit from the rich learning that takes place in an LEP classroom. Most students are not aware that they are employing a particular learning style. Fleming & Baume (2006, p. 2) note that "most students have a second modality that may be strong" and "other students may find that they use different styles in different subjects." LEP educators must be flexible, and meet each learner's needs by teaching with strategies that embrace various types of learning in the classroom as they weave LEP through the learning style preferences of all students.

The four main types of learning include, visual, auditory, reading and writing, and kinesthetic. Visual learners learn by seeing and visualizing. Visual learners prefer to see information and tend to visualize relationship between ideas. Visualization is widely used in the LEP teaching method for understanding new concepts through association and to improve memory retention. The educator can present students with visual triggers such as images that can encourage visualization of lived experiences, as it relates to the subject matter presented. Invoking words and phrases that conjure up mental pictures that relate to the content under study is also an optimal way for an educator to assist students to learn through the visual style of learning.

Auditory learners prefer to hear information rather than read it or see it displayed visually. Auditory learners are usually natural listeners. Auditory learners learn by listening and verbalizing. LEP educators can assist the auditory student by explaining or using verbal examples of their lived experiences, or use a story to explain concepts. LEP educators can employ additional tactics such as asking an oral question about a lived experience, as it relates to a concept under discussion, and calling on students to share their examples.

Learning through reading and writing are preferred learning styles among some students who prefer the information displayed as words. Students, who prefer reading and writing, learn best when interacting with the text or other written materials. Learners with a preference of the reading and writing style of learning tend to enjoy reading in all forms, and prefer information that they are learning to be displayed in the writing format. Introducing reading assignments and requiring students to complete concept LEP mind maps relating to the topic they are reading about is an excellent strategy to augment the reading and writing learning style.

Kinesthetic learners are best served by hands-on activities. Students who prefer this learning style often do better when they are involved and active. Kinesthetic learners learn by doing, they like approaches that teach them through trial and error. To utilize the kinesthetic approach, LEP educators can develop projects and activities to be discussed and solved in the classroom, or bring in items that relate to the topic under class discussion that students can touch and feel as they are learning to assimilate the new information to their existing memories.

Through its personal approach and the use of sensory memory the LEP teaching method embraces and supplements all learning styles. LEP teaching method is grounded in real world learning and as a result the brain learns efficiently making real connections between the materials being learned, and the memories of the students' lived experience. LEP learning seeks to make meaningful personal connections between the concepts under study and weave together all existing information, resources and memories to assist in the learning process of students in all learning styles.

INFUSING LEP THROUGH CONTENT, STORY, DISCUSSION, GROUP WORK, AND BLOGS

Content

Good content engages students on the onset and meets them where they are. LEP content approach to learning focuses on the personal meaning of what is being taught more so than on the content description itself. LEP teaching methods require educators to use many techniques to infuse content in a relevant way that creates an interest and an active learning environment for students to absorb and connect to the information. Infusing content in various forms such as story, discussions, group work and blogs increases student engagement and comprehension of the material. An active learning environment, especially an environment that promotes personal authentic learning, offers a stronger connection to information being learned and assists students in habits of information seeking.

Story

People love a good story. Mitch Joel contends that "it's not all about content. It's all about stories. It's not all about stories. It's all about *great* stories." Every student will learn through their own personal story because personal stories are *great* stories. The concept of story personalizes lived experience in an LEP course, and this personalization assists in comprehension of the material and places the content into long term learning. A story is an adaptive and social way to reach students and increase their learning outcomes and long-term memory. The concept of story personalizes the content and links inquisitive reflection of lived experiences to existing information and thereby creates a new story, or new information. In his book, *A Whole New Mind*, Pink (2006, p. 101) explained the concept of "story" as an integral human experience, "stories are easier to remember because in many ways, stories are how we remember." Turner (1996, p. 4-5) noted that "story is the fundamental instrument of thought," and "rational capacities depend on it. It is our chief means of looking into the future, of predicting, of planning, and of explaining….most of our experience, our knowledge and our thinking is organized as stories." Pink (2006, p. 103) further contends that "story is a high concept, because it sharpens our understanding of one thing by showing it in the context of something else." Norman (1993, p. 146) added "…stories are important cognitive events, for they encapsulate, into one compact package, information, knowledge, context and emotion." By using LEP personal stories in classroom, students are able to assimilate, and link the information being learned to their lived experiences, or other students' lived experiences, and imbed new understanding into their long-term memory.

The LEP educator should utilize reflective questions when teaching through story: Can you think of a time where you can apply this concept in your own lived experience, in your own story? Can you think of a memory of a story which can be connected to the content under study that is similar? Story discussions can be very meaningful and informative for students as they exchange information with their peers and process the topic from their unique and personal cognitive perspective. As students critically think through their lived experiences to connect to the material being learned, they are reinforcing the content in their memory because they can connect to it personally through a story, thus further imprinting learned information into long-term memory.

Discussion

Interactive communication is a draw for students. And while whole class discussions may not be conducive to covering large amounts of content, discussion should occur in every classroom because human beings learn and make memories when they share their ideas, thoughts and perceptions. Creating memories by sharing lived experiences to content under study is a way students learn and remember information long term because it is through the lived experiences of social interaction that most life meaning is derived from and memories are made.

Interactive communication and discussion gets the attention of students and they become engaged because this allows them the opportunity to interact with each other and the material in a personal way.

Classroom discussions increase students' speaking skills, often establish an easy rapport in the classroom and offer students opportunities to test their ideas, and reflections. Classroom discussions are a phenomenal learning tool where students can exchange their opinions, brainstorm, and hear the opinion of their peers. Classroom discussions create opportunities for students to share and defend their positions and sharpen many other skills, such as practice their ability to articulate their thoughts and experiences. The classroom discussion format also brings great rewards in the form of receptivity because students are more receptive to the educator, each other, and the material. Moreover, sharing experiences is vital to the student-educator relationship and can be very powerful as students are immersed in understanding how the concepts they are learning are beneficial and operate in their life and their classmates' lives.

When planning for LEP discussions in class, it is recommended that not only cognitive content aspects are considered such as determining learning outcomes from the activity, but that educators take some time to consider the social and emotional factors their students encounter, as lived experiences very often are very personal in nature. It is important not to rush the students, but give them ample time to express themselves in the discussion and to encourage participation by all students, so that each student can foster the habit of regularly sharing experiences as they relate to the content learned throughout the course.

Group Work

Group work should somehow be included in every course. "Shared learning gives learners an opportunity to engage in discussion, take responsibility for their own learning, and thus become critical thinkers" (Totten, et al. 1991, in Laal & Laal, 2012). There is no set formula for creating effective group opportunities, yet there are various effective ways and innovative approaches within the LEP teaching methods which can enhance shared learning and offer a platform for students to increase their learning outcomes, stay engaged and enjoy the course. Group work may result in spending more time on fewer topics within the textbook, but often students who work in groups develop an increased ability to solve problems quicker, learn to communicate more effectively, and have greater understanding of the material.

Within the LEP teaching paradigm, group work is vital because it allows for sharing LEP reflections with classmates in a manner that allows for knowledge to further develop and deepen. In group work students co-create and share valuable personal insights which assists the group as a whole in understanding the concepts and the concept applications to the real world, and to the students' themselves. LEP group work involves active dialogue and engagement between students to learn from and understand each other's perspectives, and creates a safe environment for learners to participate, ask questions and make mistakes without sanctions.

Ongoing dialogue, giving direction, and consistency in follow up are required of LEP educators when students are working in their groups. Especially on the onset of the first group activity, directing the group work and ensuring that students are correctly linking the concept to their lived experience, and explaining how the concept can be illustrated using real lived experiences can greatly assist students to understand the process, make their own connections and help in understanding how the concept is relevant to them.

Students should be consistently encouraged to comment about their understanding and ideas about the concept under study and share their experiences with other members of the group to either problem solve, brainstorm ideas, or provide feedback. It is important to note that group discussions should always be content oriented, even though personal lived experiences are used as a tool for understanding and memory retention. Since sharing can be personal, and often in student dialogue a conversation may take various turns away from the content under study, there may be occasions where the educator must step in and redirect the group discussion from personal experiences that do not necessarily relate to the topic at hand, back to the content under study. With every self discovery students' interest grows, and they love sharing their experiences so it is up to the educator to ensure that all discussions center on content.

The LEP group assignments planned for the course need to be carefully examined to ensure optimal learning outcomes and effectiveness of group efforts. Group work can be challenging, but issues can be eliminated or minimized if the assignments are designed optimally. For example, in group work often one or two members dominate the discussion, others withdraw; thus, an LEP group work activity sheet that every student must complete and share with the group members would eliminate or minimize this issue. An activity sheet or mind map insists that all students participate and contribute with feedback, and should include a collective understanding summary (see Activity 12 group work). This may be a onetime assignment or a larger project throughout the semester, but all students should participate.

Students may also present their group projects in an oral presentation or PowerPoint, sharing their understanding of the concept with other classmates. It is also recommended that the educator split the chapter into several sections and allow different groups to work on key concepts within their chapter section. Additionally, students should present the information to the class to increase the collective understanding of the material.

Smaller groups, rather than larger groups, work best in the LEP paradigm with 4 students per group at a maximum. Regular check in by the educator is a must for a smooth continuous flow of group work from beginning to end. To ensure that students are achieving the lesson objectives and to check for understanding, it is important for the educator to consistently observe and review the completed student LEP group work activity sheets.

Allocating time for in-class group work is crucial. Educators should not underestimate the time students will need to thoughtfully work their way through a concept, especially since reflecting on personal experiences and connecting it to content may need additional time. It is recommended that time be built into this exercise, or if it is not available, perhaps dedicate the last few minutes of class to get the students started and have them complete the assignment at an optimal time that the groups can meet independently to work on their assignment. Educators may also set aside a day that is dedicated for group work.

Since group work may be progressive, educators can ask for a quick update on the overall group's progression on the project, even if group work is not regularly scheduled during class time. In addition to regular updates, educators can have students report on their progress through a checklist of steps in the project or post a discussion board post on the internet relating to their progress. However, students need to do more than just complete group tasks; it is also important that they inquisitively reflect on the group processes and outcomes at the end of the assignment or project. By questioning what they have understood and what still remains unclear helps students to form generalized principles which then influence their future understanding and increases their point of reference as a result of the new knowledge.

Blogs

LEP student blogs are a superlative tool for students to enhance their creative learning skills and gain a deeper understanding of the material learned. Using blogs in both on-line and traditional courses not only reinforces basic writing skills but offers an opportunity for students to creatively share their experiences within the LEP platform. LEP web blogs can be designated as private or collective. Private web blogs are accessed only by the student; collective blogs are shared by the classroom and are open for posting by all students. By sharing blogs on their understanding of the content studied, students are learning from each other.

Moreover, in sharing academic progress with their classmates, according to Pahomov (2014), students can both advise and receive assistance from their peers. Pahomov (2014) continued with the idea that sharing personal achievements and understanding of the material helps those who are struggling in a similar area and assist students troubleshoot and work through problems with greater ease.

Student LEP blogs are an important way to reinforce the content under study. Maintaining a regular blog throughout their time in a course, or even blogging randomly, helps students to continually reflect on their work while it is fresh and use these reflections as a study resource to reinforce these concepts in long-term memory. Through student sharing, LEP blogs also inspire and motivate students to connect concepts to rich experiences that may have been spurned by a post from a classmate, which lead to deeper reflections. Students may use the included LEP student reflection blog (see Assessment 7) or educators may create their own to better suit their discipline demand. Consistent time spent on LEP blogging using LEP's inquisitive reflection as it applies to concepts learned in the classroom encourages students to begin to reflect more frequently and naturally in their day-to-day blogging experience.

There are a myriad of ways to work with LEP blogs. Educators can develop starter posts for their students in which to blog and allow classmates access, or they may also elect to instruct students to start their own conversations. However, students should always have an option to post their own blogs in a private setting to maintain their personal LEP reflections. Regardless of whether the blog is public or private, LEP blogging is a powerful tool for students to increase critical thinking and writing skills and to see growth within themselves and their knowledge base as they connect content to real-life applications, and see how what they are learning is operating in their life. Making guidelines clear, articulating an understandable rubric for scoring posts (if applicable) and encouraging creativity are important in the development of a successful learning LEP blog for students.

LEP blogging to reinforce new learning has had amazing results. Students are highly engaged in relating their experiences to the content under study making it a shared learning process between themselves, their classmates and the educator. LEP blogging brings forth a deeper analysis of the concept; it is much more than just recounting the activities or just an overall description of the content. Rather, it is an in-depth analysis of personal lived experiences through inquisitive reflection, the meaning of those experiences, and how they are now applied to the new concept and new learning which will not only assist in reinforcing memory but transform the way students learn. Through blogging, students can pause, reflect and think about what they are learning and informally record their thoughts about the concept under study, its relevancy in their life, and how they can use this information in the future.

CHAPTER SEVEN

IT'S PERSONAL: IMPLICATIONS FOR ONLINE LEARNING

ORGANIZING ONLINE LEARNING PLATFORM TO
INCLUDE LEP
ADDRESSING FEEDBACK TO ONLINE STUDENTS

"Online learning is not the next big thing; it is the now big thing."

—Donna J. Abernathy

Something critical is missing in online courses. That something critical is a personal connection, not just to the educator, and other classmates, but to the content. The loss of a personal touch and connection is a common complaint by students participating in online learning. Online learning has traditionally focused on content development and assessment rather than on learning deliveries that emphasize a personal touch and connectedness (Nextthought, 2016). Content development, sequencing and assessment are a good starting point in designing online courses, but educators also need to increase a personal connectedness within student learning networks (Nextthought, 2016). "We need to introduce truly personal elements into our courses, moments that have affective and communal impact... emphasizing a personal touch and overall learner connectedness" (Nextthought, 2016, p.1).

Online courses cannot remain impersonal and still engage students to their optimal learning potential. The elements of personal connections must be deployed successfully by providing a rich learning environment that allows students to share the memories of their personal lived experiences as a learning tool and memory process, which goes beyond just sharing information through online discussion boards. To boost effectiveness and student engagement, distance learning as a whole needs to embrace adding personal teaching methods to their online course design. Personal teaching does not mean a human must be present to answer all questions personally, as the mere presence of a human will not constitute higher engagement and learning outcomes, but applicably of the material learned to the students personally will increase student engagement, learning outcomes and memory retention.

ORGANIZING ONLINE LEARNING PLATFORM TO INCLUDE LEP

> *"For good ideas and true innovation, you need human interaction, conflict, argument, debate."*
>
> —Margaret Heffernan

Students lack a personal interaction in their learning process; they lack the presence of personal connection to educators and the material. Providing interactive learning opportunities in online courses is often cited as best practice by many researchers and taken very seriously by the LEP educators. LEP educators not only provide interactive learning activities in a unique way by incorporating memories of students' lived experiences as the foundation of learning and retention of learned information, but play an active role of an involved teaching presence that not only imparts information, but engages the student in active personal learning.

The LEP teaching method is the true personal connection online courses lack because it works with memories of students' personal lived experiences to frame understanding of new information. LEP teaching methods recognize that learning online is not the same as it is in a traditional classroom. In online courses, students do not have the luxury of face to face interaction and asking a question, sharing an opinion, disagreeing with a point of view, or engaging in an enlightening discussion, thus the LEP personal approach to content is a needed student centered way to offer students a new lens of understanding and making more personally authentic connections with themselves, and other learners.

In the LEP designed online courses personal connections are emphasized because the material is being learned and shared through personal means. Online students are not bored, falling asleep in their digital classes because the new information is relevant to them and has personal significance. The majority of students registered in online courses have taken many other distance learning classes, and are used to its traditional structure which usually consists of a medley of reading, lecture videos, tests, discussion posts, papers, and maybe some other type of miscellaneous homework. LEP utilizes the traditional structures but personalizes them to the student, and answers their questions as to how "this video, post, reading assignment and so on relates to me personally? What am I learning? How is this new information going to help me?"

When educators are adapting courses to online platforms that will use LEP teaching methods, they must pay careful attention to the instructional design and establish connections to content with specific LEP examples. Students, as human beings, need to feel connected to the material they are learning and feel a sense of relevancy to stay engaged; and this means even in an asynchronous setting. As a result of creating rich LEP instructional designs, the quality and patterns of communications that students practice during online learning improve, and content connections strengthen and authentic learning takes place. A rich environment promotes student interactivity and can facilitate the development of critical thinking skills, better learning, socialized intelligence, and reflection (Palloff, and Pratt, 2005, in Zygouris-Coe, 2012) in both the traditional and online settings.

To create a robust LEP learning environment at the start of the course, personal contact is essential to start a positive LEP relationship between the educator and students. If possible, educators should have the course available to students at least one week prior to the start date. At the beginning of the course, LEP educators should send students a welcome email with the course syllabus, and an overview of the LEP teaching method. The LEP's teaching approach and its benefits should be explained fully to prepare students for the expectations of the course.

In an LEP online course students must feel psychologically safe, engaged and supported, but they must also feel a degree of a personal relationship, a personal connection with the educator, one of mentoring, which goes beyond the educator as the imparter of knowledge. Thus, from the very beginning of the course the educator and the class as a whole should be encouraged to share their lived experiences as it relates to the content. Moreover, students must be made to feel comfortable enough to call forth the memories of their lived experiences to share with others and successfully make the move from content absorption to content connection using their own or their classmates' lived experiences.

In online learning platforms there are various mechanisms to keep progress reports on student online participation. Students who are not participating in using LEP should be contacted via email or a phone call to alert them that questions are welcomed, and remind them of the dangers of falling behind. This communication between the educator and student can be helpful for problem resolution and establishing supportive educator/student relationships strengthening the idea that the educator does indeed care that the student is present and participating.

To increase student engagement early in online courses utilizing LEP teaching methods the educator should initiate the first introductory posting in the discussion board. In that post, educators can introduce themselves, provide a short biography statement, and share personal lived experiences of their own. Including a picture helps to personalize the course and creates more familiarity with the educator. Students in the course should also provide an introductory post, and include any memories that relate to the course being taught, as well as information about their future goals and plans. This type of an informal discussion online promotes a community and sets up the establishment of communication between the "educator and students" and "student to student." Through this open forum, students may connect to their classmates' lives and their experiences and more personal relationships can be established.

The more personal relationships that are established between classmates, the deeper the reflections, the greater student engagement, and the more students will share their lived experiences as it relates to the understanding of the concepts. To keep things moving the educator may pose a question relating to the material or start a debate on a concept on a weekly basis, asking students to connect to the content using their LEP's inquisitive reflection thereby giving all students the opportunity to see, respond, and utilize their own LEP examples and provide their understanding of the concepts to the class as a whole. Asking students to be descriptive and share their reflections allows for superior understanding of the concept which enables students to see how the content can be connected to their own and other students' lives.

To further promote the personal aspects of LEP in learning and student engagement, the educator may also set up private online group forums. These forums are used for collaborating with other students during small group activities and are usually limited to only those members assigned to that group. In small online group forums, students can share ideas and lived experiences more privately to better understand the content, and solve problems in a safer psychological setting. In this way, they are able to see a variety of viewpoints and experiences as it relates to the material being learned. The online group forum may work together on a joint short project, or a project that is continuing throughout the course.

Additionally, educators using LEP must employ questioning techniques that will stimulate students' critical thinking skills and memory recall of lived experiences in order to successfully engage the student. Researchers (Brown & Kelley, 1986; Hemming, 2000) note the importance of integrating questioning techniques into online courses where students can demonstrate and practice critical thinking skills. LEP designed courses in an online environment using discussion boards, and written assignments should provide questions that prompt critical thinking skills and stimulate memories of students' to enhance connectivity between content and the lived experiences.

LEP students in an online course should have a mediated environment of community learners which is especially designed for shared experience. LEP teaching methods in an online format provide students with personal relevancy of what they are learning, practical experience, and a sense of belonging and accomplishment, thereby creating interest, engagement and a sense of motivation within them. Within this process, student buy-in becomes high, with increased energy, inspiration, creativity and involvement. Students approach learning and studying with greater enthusiasm and often exceed the requirements which contribute to the overall motivation of the class. The LEP teaching method is successful in distance learning because it is mentally and personally inclusive, engaging and relevant.

ADDRESSING FEEDBACK TO ONLINE STUDENTS

"Learners need endless feedback more than they need endless teaching."

—Grant Wiggins

Feedback is critical in any course, but it is especially critical in an online LEP designed course. According to *Strategies for Providing Feedback in Online Courses* (University of Illinois, 2015, p.1), "students need much more support and feedback in an online environment than in a traditional course." Feedback in online classes not only enhances the learning experience, but many researchers contend it actually makes learning possible in the first place. Using effective and consistent feedback strategies, educators can transform students' learning and meet their learning needs as well as encourage students to participate and continue to participate.

Feedback can take the form of regularly scheduled evaluations of submitted work or at the midway point of the online classes, or at any other time the educator feels necessary. Feedback should be informative throughout the online course with positive statements first, and suggestions for improvements second. It is important to remember that although the LEP teaching method is personal, feedback is not. Feedback should never be personal in nature; instead it must be constructive and encouraging.

It is imperative that online educators continue to provide to students clear and concise feedback throughout course. Because the implementation of the use of students' lived experience as a learning tool in the virtual classroom may be uncomfortable for some students at first, or confusing, feedback must be thorough and consistent to put the student at ease, and draw them out so that they can make personal connections to the content. Providing students steady feedback improves student learning, encourages, and motivate them to do better and is an essential part of learning.

An optimal way to ensure constant feedback throughout the course is for educators to set up a comprehensive framework for actionable feedback, as well as a set schedule for it in the course module. For example, online educators should consider setting virtual office hours on a weekly basis, during which time they will be available by telephone or live video chat (i.e., Skype). This is also the time to schedule phone conversations with students who may require more personal communication with the educator, who are not participating, and/or who may need additional assistance in working with the LEP paradigm. Additionally, it is critical to respond to messages and questions from students within 24 hours of receiving those inquiries. When students are motivated to achieve something they should be encouraged and have the support system to do so. For the student to stay engaged, the educator must also be interested in helping them achieve.

Constructive feedback by educators using the LEP teaching methods should be an expectation of students in an online course. It assists students to understand the concepts and gives them clear guidelines on how to improve learning. Bellon et al. (1991, p. 277) asserts that "academic feedback is more strongly and consistently related to achievement than any other teaching behavior.. this relationship is consistent regardless of age, socioeconomic status, race or school setting." Feedback can increase students' confidence, self-awareness and enthusiasm for learning (University of Reading, 2017). "Effective feedback during the first year in university can aid the transition to higher education and may support student retention" Yorke, (2002). Moreover, providing feedback should enhance learning and improve assessment performance (University of Reading, 2017).

CHAPTER EIGHT

CULTURAL AWARENESS IN TEACHING AND LEARNING

COINING A CULTURALLY DIVERSE
COLLEGE CLASSROOM
CULTURE VARIATIONS IN LEARNING PATTERNS

"Once you understand and appreciate other people's cultural backgrounds, then you can also connect with them more."

—Anonymous

Long hailed as a melting pot of cultures (Bhouraskar, 2017), the United States is home to millions of immigrants. Students are no longer a homogeneous body of traditional college age American students. In this continuously changing educational landscape educators are challenged with creating inclusive environments where students of all cultural backgrounds feel represented and welcomed. This may seem as a daunting challenge as the differences between cultures are wide spread, but students from varied nationalities, ethnicities, races, and ages, bring cultural customs, practices and varied lived experiences to their interactions. It is up to educators to recognize, celebrate, share and use these cultural variations as tools for learning.

The importance of educators being culturally aware in their classrooms cannot be overstated. For educators cultural awareness necessitates that they step out of their comfort zones and allow themselves to teach in a collaborative way, and to learn from their students. Culturally aware educators ensure that content is taught and the curriculum delivered in a manner that is responsive to the collective norms and experiences of all the students in their classroom.

COINING A CULTURALLY DIVERSE COLLEGE CLASSROOM

> *"We cannot teach what we do not know and we cannot lead where we will not go."*
>
> —Malcom X

Culture is man-made and can be used as a tool for learning. Culture is a lived experience that is unique to each individual. Culture as a lived experience encompasses all aspects of social life in any society because each society stresses certain elements in its social structures more than the others, and this forms the cultural lived experience (Ocholla-Ayayo, 1980). But culture is not just general whole societies (e.g. Italian), there are many sub cultures within cultures, for example, farmers, nurses or teenagers and so on that belong to multiple cultures at the same time (Looi, 2003). Looi (2003) further explained that there are also personal subcultures within cultures, such as the preferences in learning styles, or attitudes that must all be taken into consideration. Thus within any one culture there is much variability within students, and great care must be taken to ensure that all students are included in the learning process and meeting learning and course outcomes.

When coining a diverse college classroom sharing and collaborative learning top the list. Collaborative environments breed significantly more ideas and perceptions in which students can use as lenses to understand new material in various ways. Through interacting and sharing the concepts under study are explored in a more comprehensive, personal and memorable way. Educators are strongly encouraged in participating and sharing their culture and their lived experiences as it relates to the content they are teaching and be the example that their students are seeking. Educators should consistently encourage all students in the classroom to reach out to one another to discuss the content, solve problems and share information which will build their knowledge base and assist in storing the information in long-term memory.

The influence of culture is recognized to be a key factor in how people learn and behave (Sen, 2004). Thus, creating an environment where open and honest communication is possible so that all students have an opportunity to share cultural personal experiences as it relates to content being learned is also of utmost importance. Within a diverse classroom environment educators must impart a sense of safety where students are valued, supported and respected. Students should have the freedom and control of expressing their views and memories within the boundaries of courteous behavior. Bhouraskar (2017) noted that educators should trust and let students be free to express opinions and memories within a culturally responsive classroom, and "students will eventually tap into their humane side and find ways to understand each other." Students will still have their differences, but there will be a growing sense of acceptance, with positive learning encounters. Cultural barriers can cease to exist, and students can look beyond their differences and can focus on the common goal of learning, and understanding material from various points of view, which vastly assists in learning and retaining the material long-term.

LEP lends itself to cultural awareness and learning in the classroom because it embraces values, behaviors, beliefs, attitudes, all experiences and memories of the students and uses them as a tool for learning and memory retention. LEP is a culturally responsive teaching strategy that maximizes students' memories of lived experiences to enrich their learning regardless of their culture. LEP plays a role in how students from various cultural backgrounds can communicate with each other and receive information, and shapes their thinking and learning processes. LEP's personal approach alleviates some of the challenges facing educators in designing a learning community that is reflective of the diversity of its students because it finds ways to incorporate the students' various lived experiences, regardless of culture, in teaching the content. Culturally responsive teaching acknowledges, responds to, and celebrates fundamental cultures (Olneck, 1995), thereby prompting greater student engagement, understanding and memory retention of material being learned.

LEP culturally responsive teaching emphasizes that lived experiences can enhance learning in a multicultural environment by using an intercultural approach. The emphasis on lived experiences imparts to students the need for them to understand the perspectives of others and that of their own, and how they acquired them. LEP culturally responsive teaching helps students see the connections between experience, reflection, theory, and practical applications not only as the content applies to their own culture, but also how that same content relates to their classmates cultures which often vastly improves understanding and increases learning outcomes.

When students from different cultures share a classroom—or if the educator comes from a different culture than his/her students—it is important to consider how cultural backgrounds can affect classroom dynamics and learning. Educators are always encouraged to assess themselves for cultural assumptions or stereotypes that may be brought into the classroom, seek ways to make the classroom more culturally inclusive, and to put themselves in each of their students' shoes. For educators using LEP culturally responsive teaching with a classroom full of students from different backgrounds, the responsibility to connect with them goes beyond simply knowing where they are from. Educators must strive to understand their students in a more holistic way, sharing their own lived experiences, transcending through any biases and incorporating various cultural traditions into lesson plans and activities, so students feel understood, comfortable, and focused on learning.

CULTURAL VARIATIONS IN LEARNING PATTERNS

"It's different cultures that make the world go 'round at the end of the day."

—Samantha Fox

The different cultures of the world are representations of various human civilizations. Some cultures are vibrant and complex. Other cultures are very social, and relaxed, yet, others, more conservative, and disciplined. Each culture is rooted in its own core values and fundamentals, and educators must take into consideration the cultural dynamics and group differences in the courses they are teaching.

However, culture does not have a distinct learning pattern. Of course, life experiences and the values of a student's culture affect both the expectations and the processes of learning to a marked degree, but "researchers have clearly established that there is no single or dual learning style for the members of any cultural, national, racial, or religious group" (Dunn, 1997, pp. 74–75), but tapping into students' personal cultures in the classroom to explain content learned can enrich and increase learning experiences for all students. Sharing culture as a lived experience in learning should be encouraged and practiced as it greatly increases the understanding of concepts under study and offers a glimpse into the contents' various applications. LEP designed courses embrace culture, and educators should exemplify cultural applications to content when teaching whenever or wherever possible, and stress the importance of students using themselves as a tool for learning and sharing their culture with their classmates to explain content being learned.

Students taught in the LEP practice learn that they have unique lived experiences and unique learning patterns. This realization of their own "multiple subjectivities can help them understand the multiple and interlocking experiences of other students" (Knefelkamp, 1997, p. 3). "The classroom then becomes a living laboratory" (Knefelkamp, 1997, p. 4). Students recall their lived experiences and learn of the lived experiences of their multi-cultural classmates, and understand the concepts learned from different perspectives. As students listen and learn from each other they will become more effective learners in a multi-cultural world, and in their course work. Successful LEP educators can mine the varied memories of the students' lived experiences and use diversity as a learning tool for real and authentic learning.

CHAPTER NINE

MOVING BEYOND TRADITIONAL TEACHING

> REFRAMING EDUCATION THROUGH LEP TEACHING METHODS AND EXPLORING THE POSSIBILITIES BUILDING THE NEXT GENERATION OF LEP EDUCATIONAL LEADERS

"Educators remind us that what counts in a classroom is not what the teacher teaches; it's what the learner learns."

—Alfie Kohn

It is time to raise the bar and move beyond traditional teaching to increase student engagement and learning and course outcomes, not through a completely divergent method of teaching and learning, but through adding LEP to established methods, assumptions, practices and systems educators already use. Kohn (2000, p. 4) asserts that "learning is just the acquisition of very specific skills and bits of knowledge, a process that is linear, incremental, measurable. It says the learner should progress from step to step in a predictable sequence, interrupted by frequent testing and reinforcement with each step getting progressively more challenging." LEP helps in acquiring that knowledge and raises the bar by challenging the students to actively and progressively participate in the course work, learn and be able to apply the concepts learned to their life. LEP makes the learning journey for students exciting because of its personal association to content learned; as a result students are more effective and engaged in the course material and with enthusiasm attend class.

REFRAMING EDUCATION THROUGH LEP TEACHING METHODS AND EXPLORING THE POSSIBILITIES

Reframing the way students are taught is an essential part of educational reform and LEP teaching methods offer a new teaching initiative to affect that change. Reframing is having the insight to interpret occurrences and situations in divergent ways. It is also having the ability to choose the interpretation, solution and perspective that is optimal for the required outcome. The need for instructors to reframe teacher preparation and teaching methods from the traditional model which is memory based, to an inclusive model such as LEP teaching method, which offers unique, personalized learning and gives students the tools, techniques and the environment necessary for learning and retaining information, cannot be overstated.

To meet the demands of the LEP teaching methods, as with any other teaching method, is hard work. Educators are busy and have multiple demands in their personal and academic life solving numerous logistical issues and developing themselves to establish new definitions of teaching and learning. However, stimulating students must be included in this equation. Students must be engaged to be retained. Ways to devise LEP's inquisitive reflection as a tool for learning among the range of students in the classroom and online must be included for students to be interested, learn in new ways, see the relevance of what they are learning, and retain the information in long-term memory.

Teaching methods traditionally focus on procedures and processes where memorization of new information has the lead role, without considering the personal contexts of individual students, such the memories of lived experiences of students as learning tools. This lack of consideration can weaken the effectiveness of the educator as teacher, and increases the number of disenfranchised students. Disenfranchised students will not be retained for long.

When fully implemented, the LEP teaching methods provide essential changes in traditional approaches to learning and teaching practices to engage and retain students. LEP teaching methods, through inquisitive reflection, provides entry points into fundamentally re-conceptualizing the meaning of quality learning and memory retention. Reframing the methods and content, that is the means and meaning of teaching, provides educators with opportunities to sharpen their own teaching skills and develop better learning and memory retention skills in their students.

The challenge is not only in capturing relationships with students and providing new information but creating new relationships out of old paradigms. Educators may still teach with traditional paradigms as these frameworks have been tried, tested and proven effective. All educators have used various educational models that withstood the test of time such as Bloom's Taxonomy, but infusing LEP into the course work and allowing students to travel the unchartered territory of their lived experiences in the classroom and using these experiences to refine and develop greater clarity of the material being learned, and retain that information long term exceeds traditional methods of learning.

The LEP teaching methods do not eschew traditional methods, but expand the limits in which students learn to include a partnership strategy of shared responsibility for student learning. Just as the student must be open to personal sharing through reflection to learn, the educator must be the role model and facilitator of the lived experience for the students and must share their own personal examples, to set the tone and provide the optimal environment for LEP learning to take place. If applied correctly, the LEP teaching methods provide an immense learning experience that is relevant to the student and taps into the student's real world and memories, which trigger student engagement and productivity.

LEP teaching methods, through inquisitive reflection, provide a means of reframing learning in substantial and important ways. LEP is demographically friendly, where age, culture, education, social or economic status are all equal learning tools, as the understanding of concepts is filtered through a personal cognitive processing that is unique to each individual increasing comprehension and memory retention. The problems and solutions are seen through a personal perspective and understood through a personal understanding. Understood from a personal viewpoint, the information is assimilated with prior memories, and expanded to include the new information; thus forming a stronger bond in comprehension and memory.

LEP learning enables irreversible, profound change for the better—in information seeking, information connection, student engagement and memory retention. The LEP teaching method addresses and explores core values, world views, beliefs, perspectives, understandings, personal patterns, existing knowledge and frameworks; in other words, it is interested in lived experience of the students and their "meaning schemes" that the students' use for thinking and imagining. These schemes through LEP's inquisitive inquiry are easily applied to memory when learning new content to transform learning from just "content absorption" to "content connection" which leads to memory retention.

The LEP teaching method is the vehicle of change within the current higher education system that improves student engagement, retention and learning outcomes and increases memory retention of learned material, thereby reflecting more effecting teaching and learning. Observable data can be seen in student engagement and attendance, evaluations and assessments, and overall course retention with increased learning outcomes. Reframing education through LEP teaching methods offers hope and possibilities for all educators to enhance their teaching quality and foster engagement on all levels of student performance—from those deemed academically at risk to those designated as honor students.

BUILDING THE NEXT GENERATION OF LEP EDUCATIONAL LEADERS

LEP teaching methods offer educators an opportunity to become a positive force for educational change, and increase student learning, engagement and in school retention. The qualities of an LEP educational leader mirror qualities of other educational leaders using other methods, with a slight deviation. The inclusion of inquisitive reflection through LEP in learning is a fresh approach that makes material relevant to students, offers real-life applications, enhances students' creativity, critical thinking skills, and increases understanding, learning outcomes and memory retention because the student is infused with an authentic and highly personal learning experience.

In this scenario, LEP educators are more than just people who helps students acquire knowledge, but are active participants guiding their students' personal learning. LEP educators work tirelessly to create challenging, trusting, and nurturing environments for their students in which to learn. LEP educators are not just subject matter experts who exhibit expertise in the subjects they are teaching, but are inspirational leaders who must inspire, arouse and enthuse a diversified range of students and engage them in the material presented.

Many factors play a role in the effectiveness and performance of educators. Academic and course credentials, knowledge, experience, critical thinking, and other aspects of intelligence, along with good communication and listening skills, are essential to be effective as an educator. Friendliness and congeniality in a supportive and collaborative environment where the educator is approachable are also effective in putting students at ease and will lead to better communication, and ultimately a better learning environment with increased learning outcomes.

Often the difference between an effective teacher and a high-performing teacher is the mindset to achieve high learning, to think out of the box, and be creative.

In an age of scripted lessons and administrative accountability creative thinking is taking a back seat. However, Pink (2005) notes that creative thinking is increasingly necessarily in today's world. Sanders and Rivers (1996) concluded that the most important factor affecting student learning is the teacher; thus it only makes sense to utilize LEP teaching methods, a creative teaching strategy with highly effective results to enhance teaching practices of educators and move from effective to high-performing teaching practices.

Effective LEP educators improve their teaching through expanding the power of students' memories to be used as learning tools in the classroom. LEP educators broaden their students' thoughts and understanding and instill the power of reflective practice in their learning. The practice of LEP's inquisitive reflection in the classroom can take an effective teacher to high performance and uncover hidden treasures, possibilities and tools that can be used to infuse new life in old course work, learning and teaching approaches.

LEP educators are skilled at providing opportunities for students to take on both ownership and leadership roles in their very personal learning which vastly increases student engagement, and retention. LEP educators have the ability to turn their personal interests and creativity into valuable teaching techniques, and weave in personal interests, and their lived experience, to student learning and problem solving. For example, a math teacher with an interest in history can integrate history into math word problems and math vignettes, and use these personal examples to explain and solve the problem.

LEP educators are highly inclusive, having complete regard for the progress and personal development of each student. LEP educators must also be self-aware, have an understanding of themselves and have the confidence to use LEP's inquisitive reflection freely to tap into their own memories and memories of their students to assist in the understanding and memory retention of the content. Having a clear vision of how LEP will be applied in the classroom and ways to promote fruitful opportunities for learning must be planned out well in advance.

LEP educators must show confidence in the LEP inquisitive reflection techniques to trigger the students to follow the educators' lead. By speaking positively of the immense results that can be attained by using the LEP process, students will acquire a belief in it as well and use it to their full advantage. The LEP educator should have consistent high expectations and demonstrate how LEP is an advantage to students' learning achievements and how their past lived experience is a valuable learning tool. Continuously communicating with students is of vital importance. Talk to your students; a good educational leader cannot lead without interaction from their followers. Interact with your students as much as possible and always be the example.

High-performing educators know that they must reach students in diverse ways. LEP is the power that allows high-performing teaching to reach all students. LEP teaching methods allows for the magic of learning to be engaging, fun and memorable with new learning curves at every opportunity as students are affected in their own unique way and are able to process new material through their personal perception and prior frameworks.

LEP educators must focus relentlessly and continually on improving teaching and learning through LEP. The LEP educator must be robust and rigorous in terms of self-evaluation and data analysis with clear strategies for improvement. Students are hungry to learn, but learning must be relevant to them if they are to be engaged and retained. Thus the LEP educator must be skilled in turning around challenges, obstacles and mind blocks and work relentlessly on behalf of students to motivate and inspire them to use LEP to meet their learning outcomes.

High performing LEP educators create a positive change in the educational system, in their students and in themselves. By showing a passion for the material being taught and creatively using LEP's inquisitive reflection in their coursework LEP educators will inspire their students to want to learn more, and show them the relevancy of the material to their lives, which results in increased student engagement, retention and learning outcomes. Set high expectations, as it greatly affects achievement; be creative, motivated and sustained by the knowledge that "teaching is a profession that makes all other professions possible."

CHAPTER TEN

Assessments

> LEP and Tests
> LEP Assessment Examples

Assessments are an integral part of instruction because they determine if the course and learning objectives are being met. According to Linn and Miller (2005) assessment is any of a variety of procedures that obtains information in relation to students' performance. Educators trust these assessments because of their direct association to instructional goals, learning and course outcomes. Nationwide assessments are designed to rank order schools and students and are for the purposes of accountability, but Guskey, (2003) asserts that assessments designed for ranking are generally not ideal instruments to assist educators to improve or modify their instruction or their teaching approach as it applies to individual students.

Another key problem with traditional assessments is that they are typically given at the end of the term or school year, when most instructional activities are completed or are near completion. Barton (2002) and Kifer (2001) contend that there are several problems with this practice. Educators do not receive the results until sometime later, meaning that although the findings may help a fresh crop of students, they cannot help the current students, and the results that are forwarded to educators usually lack the detail needed to target definite improvements (Barton, 2002; Kifer, 2001).

That leaves educators seeking ways to assess their own courses, while they are still in progress, in a way that is meaningful and beneficial to them and their current students. However, Guskey (2003) contends that despite the importance of assessments in education, few teachers receive adequate formal training in assessment design or analysis. Educators, instead, rely heavily on the assessments offered through the publisher of their textbook or other pre-made instructional materials from various sources. This process treats assessments as evaluation mechanisms to dispense when instructional activities are completed, and/or to use primarily to ration students grades (Guskey, 2003).

LEP teaching methods subscribe to a different school of thought when it comes to the traditional assessments. LEP assessments, as all assessments, are designed with a specific purpose in mind; however, they are not so much focused on accountability, but increasing current student engagement and learning outcomes. Within LEP teaching methods, classroom assessment is more than just measuring grade point averages or percentages, and whether the student was satisfied with the course or not. When properly developed and interpreted, LEP assessments are very beneficial in improving current instruction and getting a better handle on what students are learning in real-time, and whether that learning is encoded in their long-term memory.

LEP educators do not rely on cookie cutter assessments to assess their courses, nor do they delay assessment until the end of the semester or year. Highly effective LEP educators start each term with their own assessment of the course, the students and their learning, and continue the assessment process throughout the term so that they can better understand and address student and course learning outcomes while they still have the same students in the course. Guskey (2003, p. 5) contends that "teachers who develop useful assessments, provide instruction, and give students second chances to demonstrate success can improve their instruction, and help student learn." At the same time, educators who assess their classes at regular intervals greatly improve their own courses throughout the term and semester, have an opportunity to help current students, and still be able to use this information to reflect after the course is over with greater expansion.

The benefits of assessments are many. Assessments are revealing, and often the findings lead to improvements that are beneficial and effective for all parties. Various examples of LEP assessments have been included in the book, but the educator should always begin the term with the LEP general concept mind map (see Assessment 1) to help familiarize the students with the LEP processes when with working with LEP. By sharing the LEP concept map with students, the educator is providing an illustration of the process as a whole which students can visually follow in their practice of learning and remembering concepts through LEP.

Students should regularly complete the LEP test review activity (see Assessment 2) to ensure that they are fully prepared to take tests or complete their assignments. Another valuable assessment for students includes the LEP student self assessment (see Assessment 3) which places the focus on the students' effort, reasoning, and application of the concept. The self-assessment activity is very important because it allows students to self assess in a more private setting and gauge the understanding of what they are learning, in a quiet time environment where they can honestly reflect on their personal effort.

Other example assessments included in the book to evaluate student learning through LEP include an oral assessment (see Assessment 4) and the writing components assessment (see Assessment 5) which are so important in every course. The book also includes an educator's instructional assessment for inquisitive reflective blogging (see Assessment 6) which allows educators to reflect on the effectiveness of the LEP blogs and technology use in their courses and make improvements. Student blogging assessment criteria which outlines the requirements and expectations of the blogging assignment for the student (see Assessment 7) is also included and will assist the educator in evaluating students' LEP blogging progress. Moreover, educators should utilize the instructional end of term Formative LEP Course Results for Educators Assessment (see Assessment 8) to give educators an opportunity to access each course and look for improvements for the future.

All assessments should support student learning first and foremost. Thus it makes sense to stay focused on continual checks in the current classroom for student understanding, which assist educators to make informed decisions as to how to improve their teaching strategies. The greatest benefit of including assessments through LEP mind maps and concept maps is that the educator has an immediate visual idea and can gauge the students' level of understanding relating to the concept under study. Students who have a firm understanding of a concept can easily complete a concept mind map by creating meaningful patterns and connections and apply them to the relevancy of the concept in their learning and in their life.

It is worthy of note that LEP assessments are assessments "for" learning, not necessarily "of" learning. All assessments and mind mapping activities provided in this book were intentionally designed as basic, outlining only the thought processes, to allow them to be a blank canvas for the educator to structure, customize and organize to their discipline specifications. It is advised that assessments are used throughout the duration of the term to improve learning outcomes for all students in the course.

LEP AND TESTS

LEP as test review: Timing is crucial in test taking. However, preparing for tests with each review can also be vital in the eventual outcome of a test grade. A series of small LEP activities can greatly enhance the students' interest in the material that needs to be reviewed for tests.

Often educators administer extensive examinations covering several chapters. Doyle (2008) asserts that an effective practice that promotes deep student learning is the use of cumulative examinations to be utilized to retest foundational concepts, such as later in the semester or as in the time of finals. Such an approach to student testing motivates students and increases long-term memory retention. Each time the students move through the chapters in the course, and consistently note concepts in each chapter and pertinent information from lectures in the LEP test study guide activity sheet, the material will be reinforced in the long-term memory.

The LEP activity sheets will become very beneficial to study for finals if used in a continuum. They can also be an excellent source of information that can be used in research papers, critiques, and so on or for future reference. Some students may prefer to utilize the LEP test review activity, not as a continuum throughout the course, but as a one-time study test review. In that case the student would complete the LEP activity sheet in preparation for the test and include key concepts from their instructor's direction, and use it as a one-time test study guide. Utilizing LEP activities also allows students the opportunity to plan ahead for exams and master these concepts before the test occurs. LEP test activities keep students focused and allow them to review and discover strengths and weaknesses of their understanding of the material and their memory.

One of the best test reviews for students is to ask them to bring their previously taken test to class. Ask students to review their tests and rework them to include a lived experience that connects to that concept. Reworking tests increases and retains the information in the long-term memory. This is especially useful when students are studying for finals, as previous tests tend to be study guides for the final exams.

LEP ASSESSMENT EXAMPLES

Assessment 1

It is recommended that the LEP concept mind map be utilized within the first few weeks of the course to help familiarize the students with the LEP processes when with working with LEP. The educator must review the map with the students by providing concrete examples for each step.

LEP Concept Mind Map

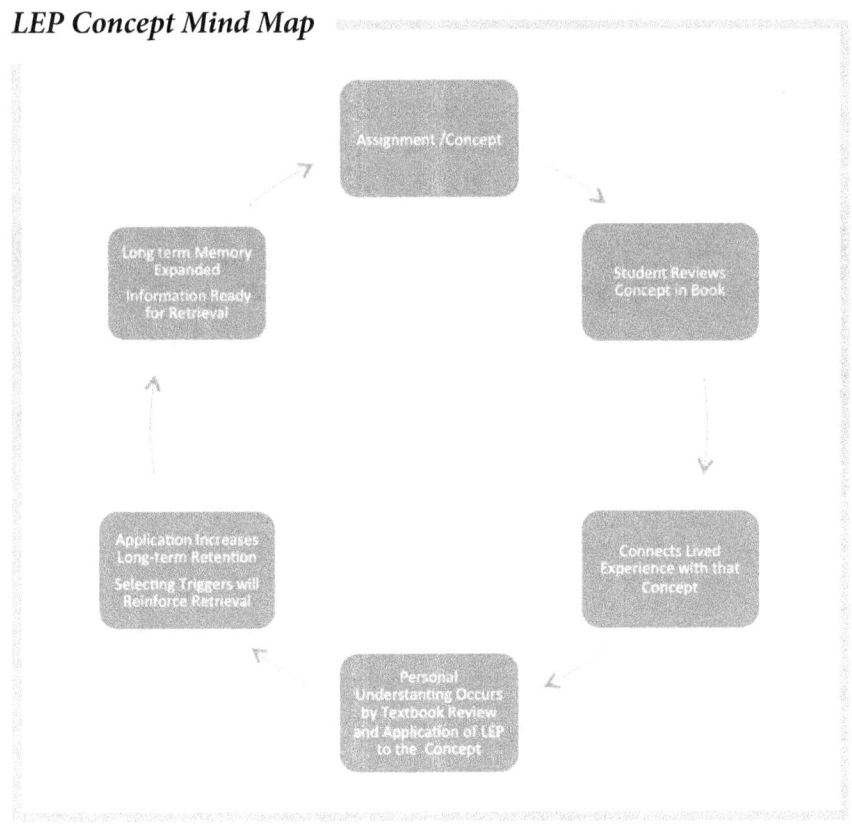

Assessment 2

STUDENT KNOWLEDGE ASSESSMENT FOR TEST PREPARATION

Directions for students to assess their learning: Students should review each chapter and note important concepts in the table below. Connect the concept to a lived experience from your life that reflects how that concept *operates* in your life. The first entry will name the concept being learned. The second entry provides the book interpretation. The third entry uses critical thinking skills to inquisitively reflect on a lived experience that directly relates to the concept and assists in a deeper personal understanding of the topic. Please reflect deeply on how the concept applies to your life and increases your understanding of the concept. Lastly, apply a trigger that will help you remember the information. During tests or during any review when you see the concept, remember to visualize the trigger, for quicker memory retrieval. (Students should regularly assess their knowledge and understanding of the subject matter they are learning by using assessment 2).

CONCEPT OR TOPIC	BOOK INTERPRETATION	LIVED EXPERIENCE	TRIGGER

Assessment 3

Concept _____

STUDENT UNDERSTANDING - LEP SELF-ASSESSMENT

	3 POINTS	2 POINTS	1 POINTS	COMMENTS
Effort: Does the worksheet reflect effort on your (student's) part to review study and understand the concept using LEP?	My work reflects great effort.	I put some effort into the work.	I put little or no effort into the work.	
Understanding: Do you (student) understand the concept you are studying?	I have a very good understanding of the concept.	I have some understanding of the concept.	I do not have an understanding of the concept.	
Connection: Have you (student) logically linked the concept to a lived experience for meaning? Can you interpret it to your understanding? Reflect on the meaning.	I am able to logically connect the concept to my lived experience resulting in new meaning for me.	I am somewhat able to logically connect the concept to my lived experience, and it has some meaning for me.	I am unable to logically connect the concept to my lived experience, and it does not hold meaning for me.	
Explanation: Can you (student) clearly explain and apply the concept as you understand it using your LEP experience.	I am easily able to explain or describe, and apply the concepts as understood through my LEP.	I am only somewhat able to explain or describe and apply the concepts as understood through my LEP.	I am unable to explain or describe and apply the concepts as understood through my LEP.	
Completion	I completed the assignment without difficulty.	I completed the assignment with some difficulty.	I was unable to complete the assignment.	

Assessment 4

QUICK ORAL LEP ASSESSMENT

[Communication]

Oral Expression

Student is verbally expressing him or herself with clarity and is making logical links between the stated definition of the concepts and their LEP.

YES__ NO__ SOMEWHAT__

COMMENTS:

Teacher ⇔ Student

Student ⇔ Student

Oral Connection

Student is verbalizing a correct understanding of the concept. Classmates (listeners) are making the connection between the concepts and LEP and have gained clarity, understanding, and the essence of the concept's meaning and its applications.

YES__ NO__ SOMEWHAT__

COMMENTS:

Assessment 5

LEP Writing Assessment

	LEP Writing Assessment				
Criteria	5 = Excellent	4 = Good	3 = Fair	4 = Poor	Comments
Overall writing at college-level structure, punctuation and grammar					
Writing introduces the concept, and provides a basic overview of the concept.					
Writing makes clear connections between the concept and the student's LEP.					
Writing presents a clear understanding of concept integrating both the concept and LEP to create meaning.					
Writing reflects meaningful and/or significant thought with a logical conclusion and summary.					

Assessment 6

EDUCATOR LEP BLOG ASSESSMENT

Course #

Since more and more students are taking online courses, many educators have turned to blogs to enhance personal learning. In order to improve the blogging experiences of students, educators should periodically assess their blogging strategies. Asking questions, could this blog strategy be better? How? What steps should I take to improve this lesson plan which will take the demographics and the needs of the students in this course into consideration? Am I satisfied with the learning outcomes of my students for this particular lesson when I read the blogs? Am I satisfied with how my students are using their LEP blog to connect to the content? What did I learn from this experience, and how can improve the blogging experience for my students?

LEP Reflection Blog #1:

LEP Reflection Blog #2

LEP Reflection Blog #3

Assessment 7

LEP INQUISITIVE REFLECTION STUDENT BLOG ASSESSMENT (RUBRIC)

LEP INQUISITIVE REFLECTION STUDENT BLOG RUBRIC CRITERIA			
3 = EXCEEDS EXPECTATIONS	**2 = MEETS EXPECTATIONS**	**1 = BELOW EXPECTATIONS**	**COMMENTS**
Entries show reflective thought, depth of clarity, and correct understanding and application of LEP as it relates to content.	Entries show reflective thought and correct application with adequate depth, understanding and application of the content taught.	Entries do not show reflective thought or adequate depth, understanding or application of the content taught.	
Entries reflect meaningful and/or significant thought, the inclusion of a well thought out trigger to remember the concept, and end with a logical conclusion and summary.	Entries reflect adequate and or meaningful thought, and an adequate trigger, and end with a logical conclusion and summary.	Entries do not reflect adequate or meaningful thought, do not mention a trigger and do not end with a logical conclusion and summary.	

Assessment 8

INSTRUCTOR END OF TERM FORMATIVE LEP COURSE ASSESSMENT

Course Name and Number : _____

Enrollment # _____

RATE THE COURSE

Assessment for Collective LEP Course Progress

Collective classroom progress should be assessed after each course, and all LEP activity mind maps and exercises should be modified to increase intellectual competencies of the students.

LEP INTELLECTUAL COMPETENCIES:

Reading		Speaking		Critical Analysis		Reflective Analysis		Working Independently
Writing		Listening		Content Application		Comprehension		Working Collaboratively

The students increased their critical thinking and reflection skills through a personal lens and were able to connect content to lived experiences:

❏ Considerably ❏ Somewhat ❏ Not at all

COMMENTS:

The students increased application thinking through LEP's inquisitive reflection to gain purposeful meaning:

❏ Considerably ❏ Somewhat ❏ Not at all

COMMENTS:

The students increased their long-term memory and thinking skills.

❑ Considerably   ❑ Somewhat   ❑ Not at all

COMMENTS:

<u>**Overall the students showed increase in their learning outcomes:**</u>

❑ Considerably   ❑ Somewhat   ❑ Not at all

COMMENTS:

In this course class retention throughout the course:

❑ Increased   ❑ Stayed the same   ❑ Decreased

COMMENTS:

Course outcomes: Were course outcomes met? What were the weaknesses in this course as it relates to the LEP teaching method? What did not work? What needs the greatest attention and improvement?

COMMENTS:

What were the strengths in this course as it relates to the LEP teaching method? What worked well that you will expand on and improve for even greater effectiveness?

COMMENTS:

CHAPTER ELEVEN

INSTRUCTIONAL MIND MAPPING ACTIVITIES AND HELPFUL HANDOUTS

ACTIVITY 1

LEP INQUISITIVE REFLECTION MIND MAPPING

It is recommended to take part in rhythmic breathing to settle, clear and refocus the mind. Rhythmic breathing balances the body and clears the mind enough to proceed. There are many variations of breathing techniques, but usually breathing in for eight counts, holding for eight counts, and releasing for eight counts quiets the mind. Each set of eight should be repeated three to five times.

The student must be mentally prepared to inquisitively reflect and have a quiet place to do so. It is *not* uncommon for strong emotions to surface as the mind explores memories as connected to the concepts being learned. At first having difficulty concentrating may occur, but students are to be made aware that often this is expected and that with practice this process will become innate. Students are to redirect their focus to the topic at hand and how this experience serves them in understanding the concept for learning purposes. It is important to note that the student is not just exploring the moment in their mind but reliving the moment in that time, space and place. Reliving LEP and connecting the experience as it unfolds in relation to the concept under study manifests in a much deeper and richer interpretation and understanding of the material, and greatly assists in memory retention.

Tone of Meditation

Quiet the mind, but breathe naturally. (To quiet the mind LEP utilizes contemplation through meditation). Meditation trains the mind the way physical fitness trains the body. The intention is to silence all thoughts by ignoring everything that does not have to do with exploration of the connection of the content to the student's existing frame of understanding (lived experience). Meditation should be 15-30 minutes per concept. If the mind wanders it must be brought back to the content. Relax, and visualize lived experiences that may be connected, as visualization will interrupt the assault of thoughts that randomly affect focus, and use all senses to once again link content to memories of lived experiences for framing your understanding of the concept.

Inquisitively Reflect

In meditative mode, reflectively and objectively explore your memories to link them with concepts being learned. Reflect by connecting personal philosophies, lived experiences, and your current knowledge of the concept. Do not rush the process, but investigatively reflect. Have I seen this before? Have I experienced something similar? What existing framework or understanding do I already have about this concept? How can I connect this concept to my lived experience so that I can understand it better, and see how this information is relevant in my life?

The inquisitive reflection phase examines situations, events, feelings, emotions, personal knowledge, and existing information as it pertains to content learned and offers opportunities to use critical thinking to find old patterns and entertain new ways of thinking and review past decisions, actions or situations as it relates to the concept being learned. Probing and questioning during reflection are critical and are strongly encouraged.

Contemplate and Find Relevance

Through contemplation carefully consider the memories selected by your mind through inquisitive reflection, and find relevance in this information. Why was this memory selected over others to connect to the concept? Why is this information important to you? How can you use it in the future?

Relevant information means that something is interesting, and useful. Relevant and meaningful connections activate the learning process. Students are encouraged to gauge the relevance of the material they are learning, as this helps students see how the content fits into their current framework, and future point of reference. Students should not rush this process but immerse themselves in the efforts to see how this information can serve them in their existing personal framework, and in the future.

Create New Meaning

Creating new meaning from established forms of reference and frameworks: After contemplation organize thoughts so that new or different learning from existing information as it relates to the content under study is facilitated. New meaning comes from the integration of textbook understanding of the concept and personal LEP memories which expand understanding of the concept and shows its various applications for a clearer interpretation which assists in expansion of knowledge and students' growth. By assigning new meaning and assimilating information memory is reinforced. LEP meaning schemas change all the time as people add and assimilate new learning to existing schemas to expand their knowledge and understanding.

Memory Trigger

Relevant, meaningful learning engages students emotionally and connects with their existing knowledge which assists in building neural connections and long-term memory storage: Create a mental memory of the lived experience and how it related to the concept and write down the information. Review the information at various intervals, as repetition and visualizations are effective forms of learning. Once the information is assimilated and rooted in memory, choose a personal trigger that will be solely connected to the concept to remember the information. The trigger must be closely related to the concept, and all senses, personality traits, humor or any other LEP experience can be used as a trigger to recall the needed information. Be in the moment when encoding personal trigger to memory, this will set the stage to evoke the trigger when the information is needed. Triggers help remind the brain where the information is stored thereby recall is easier.

ACTIVITY 2

LEP Inquisitive Reflection Critical Thinking Skills Mind Map

Directions: This assignment utilizes critical thinking skills to visually gain mastery of the concepts under study. Select a concept from the textbook or lecture and complete the following activity sheet.

CONCEPT: is an organizing principle or mental construct that represents information. What concept are you trying to understand? What do you know about it?
CONCEPT CONNECTION AND TRIGGER: Connect concept to lived experience and create a trigger. Why did the concept make you think of this experience?
EFFECT/ACTION: What happened during this experience? What are your feelings toward the experience?
RELATION TO CONCEPT: How does your experience and what happened relate to the concept?
CREATE A TRIGGER: Use this information to create a trigger that will assist you to remember the concept.
NEW UNDERSTANDING: Based on the textbook experience and your own personal LEP investigative inquiry of the concept, what is your new understanding of the concept? How can you apply it in your life or use this information in the future?

ACTIVITY 3

LEP TASK IN-CLASS ACTIVITY

Short Task:

- In class for 5 minutes have the students reflect on a particular concept you have just lectured about and then write down their understanding of this concept as seen through their lived experience for new understanding and meaning. The explanations could be theoretical, practical, or both. Prepare the students to share them with others, if time allows. Educators may want to capture some thoughts or any ideas for later discussions. Short tasks can be used as a great class ender to review key concepts or even a class beginner to introduce new concepts for framing. The educator may introduce a concept to the class and prime students with examples of their own experience as it relates to the concept.

- **Interviews:** A teacher can interview a student or students can interview classmates to share reflections about the content as it relates to their LEP. Set aside time at the end of a learning sequence for students to interview each other about the concepts learned and how they can apply the new learning to their lives. Students should also share their lived experience that best describes a scenario that relates to the concept under study for greater understanding and memory retention. Interviews assist students with opportunities to practice a variety of beneficial communication habits such as listening with understanding and empathy and communicating effectively, using their critical thinking skills.

- Variations on above, set aside the last 10 minutes of class time for class journal. Have students write about a concept/s they have learned and apply it their lived experience to serve in better understanding and applications of the content.

ACTIVITY 4 (FOR EDUCATOR)

EDUCATOR PREPARATION CHECKLIST FOR LEP

Every educator must be aware of how the material being taught relates to the student's life. The material must be relevant and clear for student engagement. When expecting student buy-in, educators must be prepared to share their personal experience. Educators should prepare two or three LEP examples and connect them to the concept or topic being learned to include within class discussion or post the information in the discussion board section of courses with online components. Personal interaction is mandatory for successful outcomes by both the student and educator.

PLAN EARLY AND WELL. The importance of planning early for your course and having all the materials needed in class and available is crucial to optimal learning. Being organized and well structured in your planning will greatly assist in the smooth learning experiences of your students. Know the vital points that must be addressed in the class and plan to adjust LEP strategies as the course progresses, which may happen as a result of varied demographics of the class. This can be achieved through lecture formats, which include LEP examples, class discussions, written assignments or group work, or any other teaching format the educator prefers. Educators should have content LEP activities available early in the course for students to work and practice with. Additionally, educators should complete the LEP activities themselves so that they can experience the process they are asking their students to follow. This may assist in some modification of the activity sheet that the educator may deem to be necessary to suit their specific discipline.

CREATE AN ACTIVE LEARNING ENVIRONMENT AND BUILD A CLASSROOM COMMUNITY WHERE PERSONAL EXPERIENCES CAN BE SHARED TO AID UNDERSTANDING OF MATERIAL PRESENTED. Educators should find ways to make students comfortable while sharing their LEPs as they relate to the content under discussion. An active and supportive learning environment promotes stronger connection to material being learned, and an open and caring attitude and consistent behavior that promotes an environment of trust will assist in promoting a positive learning environment.

EDUCATOR TAKES THE ROLE OF FACILITATOR AND MONITOR. The educator takes the lead, sets the examples, and directs the learning process. Educators must be prepared to facilitate, mediate and monitor classroom discussions and group work allowing room for expressions, but must always be on hand to redirect the discussion to focal points of content to assist with allotted classroom time and topic. In the classroom setting all students should have the opportunity to participate and explain why they chose a certain LEP to connect to the textbook concept, as this will reinforce memory, and create an opportunity for students to share how they think this information is relevant and will serve them.

ACTIVITY 5

LEP: IT'S PERSONAL—ENCONDING MIND MAP

Encoding is the first step to creating a new memory. Memory encoding allows information to be converted into an understandable construct by placing it in categories in which students can understand and makes sense of. To properly encode a memory, paying attention is integral. Upon receipt of new content the student should encode the information in their memory by exploring their memories and selecting the appropriate category (see below) in which to understand the concept. Once a category is identified the student must "encode" the new information in the brain by associating the content with one of the selected categories and merge it with their existing knowledge. In this way existing and new knowledge is integrated, assimilated and expanded. Once encoded, the selected trigger will be used, as a cue, to retrieve that particular information from memory.

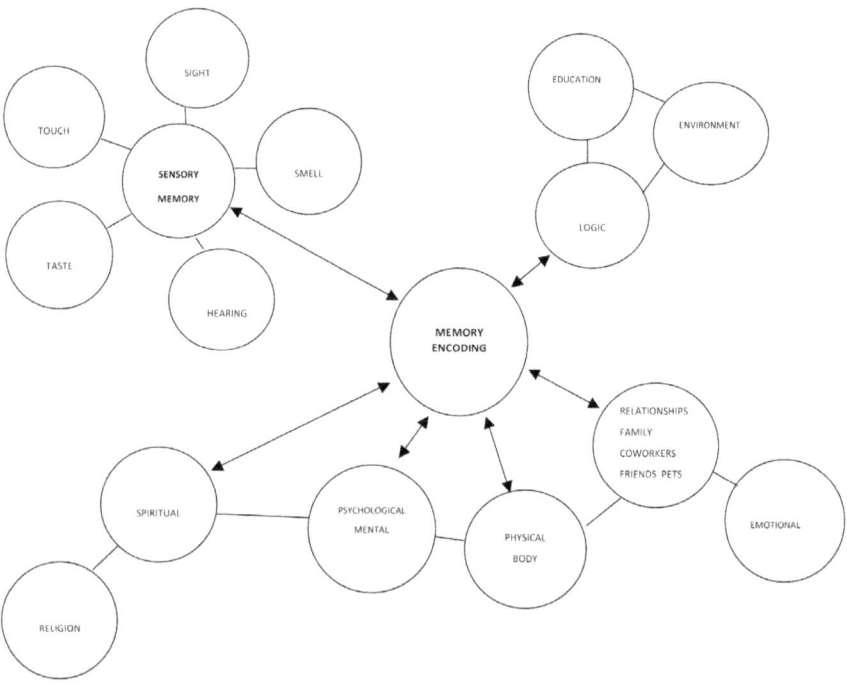

ACTIVITY 6

LEP FRAMING PROCESS

The educator should assist students in understanding the process of framing to enable them to form generalizations that link the concept with LEP. Very often using an example to frame the concept for the student in advance assists in faster connections to their LEP and expanded understanding of the concept.

Framing is a feature of our brain's structural design mechanism. Human minds react to the context in which something is embedded and tries to find patterns or existing blue prints to create meaning. To frame a concept through LEP's inquisitive inquiry, the students search their memories for an event or a situation that most closely resembles the concept definition under study. Once a lived experience is identified, the students focus on the relationships between their current understanding of the concept and the main ideas and details of their lived experience. There is an unfolding of patterns and structures from exploration of the lived experiences as they are related to new concepts as the framing begins, which is followed by meaning.

LEP FRAMING

- **FRAMING:** Frame the concept under study using your thoughts, memories and ideas in conjunction with inquisitive reflection. Approach framing as an open-ended process with existing information reframed regularly to accommodate and assimilate new information.

- **FRAMING ORGANIZES AND COLLECTS INFORMATION:** Think about exactly what you already know about the concept and write it down. How and in what capacity does the lived experience relate to the concept? Describe the event: what were the significant factors? Why did you think of this particular experience to frame the understanding of this concept? Write down the factors that relate to the lived experience and use those experiences and factors to frame the concept to give it meaning.

- **FRAMING FOR UNDERSTANDING:** Framing sets the context for understanding your concept. Framing exists to help people make sense of their world and influences how the concept is interpreted and the meaning that is assigned to them. Knowing what types of frames were constructed and why they were constructed can shed further insight relating to the understanding and interpretation of the concept under study.

- **FRAMING FOR SYNTHESIZING:** Synthesis is not just a summary of your concepts but includes deep inquisitive reflections that produce deep insights. Thus ensure that your framing activity includes more than just a summary, but also includes well thought-out-understanding and interpretation of the concept and its connection and application to your life.

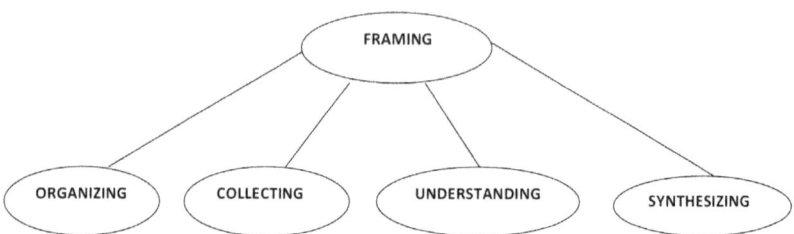

ACTIVITY 7

MEMORY SELF-TEST

Directions: Read the memory descriptions below to assess your memory profile.

Place a check in the box that best describes your memory skills.

Never = 0, Sometimes = 1, Often, = 2, Always = 3

	NEVER	SOMETIMES	OFTEN	ALWAYS
1. I am able to easily recall information learned within the last 24 hours.				
2. I remember information for short periods of time.				
3. I am able to remember information for long periods of time.				
4. I can recall much of the information I have learned in school in previous years.				
5. When studying I can remember and can easily recall the important facts.				
6. I can remember my past lived experiences and life events.				
7. I have to write things down in order to remember them.				
8. I have to try hard if I need to remember something.				
9. I use specific memory techniques such repetition to remember.				
10. I have to spend considerable amount of time studying to remember something.				

Self Scoring:
20-30: You have excellent memory
10-19: Your memory is sufficient but improvement is needed.
0-10: Your memory is not sufficient and needs improvement.

ACTIVITY 8

CLASSICAL CONDITIONING MIND MAPPING ACTIVITY

Identify a lived experience that conditioned you without your conscious efforts. If you have been bitten by a dog, you may experience fear at the sight of a dog heading in your direction. Whenever you hear a certain song, a wave of sadness may overcome you if the song was a favorite in a relationship that may have gone bad. A smell of a certain perfume brings back a specific memory from the past. Connect those memories to the content. For example, if you are learning about Italy, and your mouth waters at the smell of Italian food, connect that experience to the content learned and use a trigger to easily retrieve the content from memory when needed. Be creative!

ACTIVITY EXAMPLE

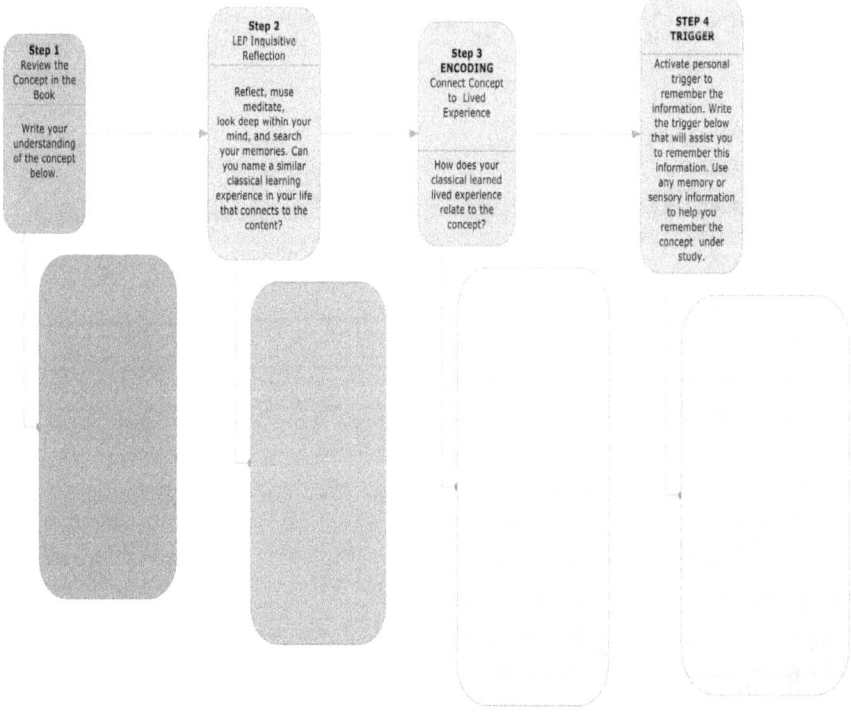

ACTIVITY 9

OPERANT CONDITIONING MIND-MAPPING ACTIVITY

Identify a lived experience that influenced you to either repeat the behavior because of some type of reward or weaken the possibility of repeating the behavior because of the consequences. Once you identify an experience, link the experience to content being learned to assist in new understanding of how that concept operates in your life.

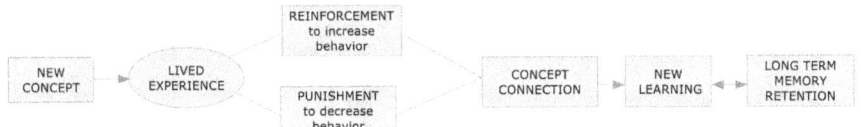

ACTIVITY EXAMPLE

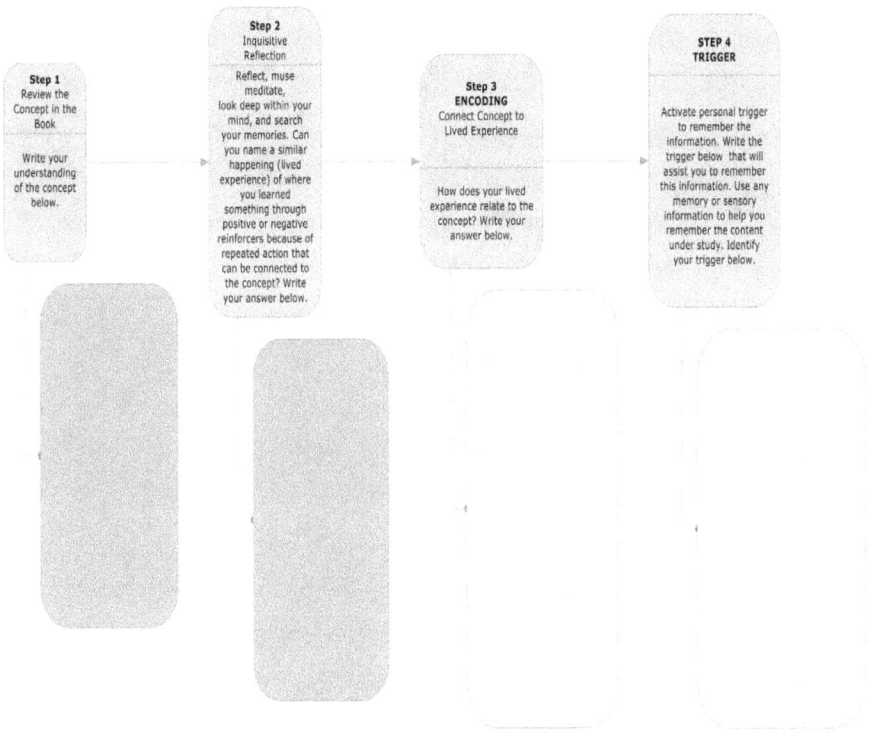

ACTIVITY 10

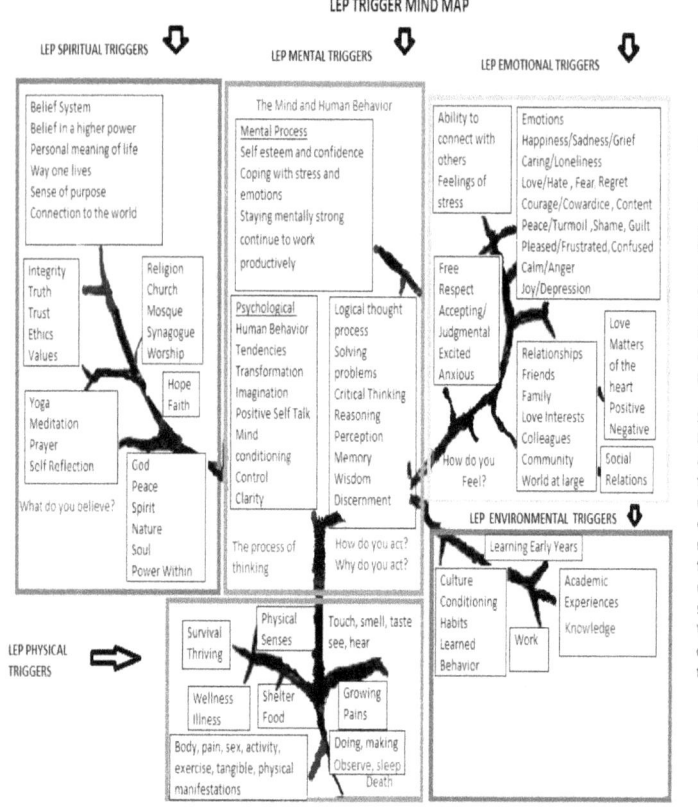

ACTIVITY 11

CREATIVE VISUALIZATION AS A CONCEPT MEMORY REINFORCER

The role of silence and a quiet place: Clearing the mind preparation. Any stressors and preoccupations can negatively impact content absorption, content connection and memory retention. Before engaging in learning, the students should clear their mind of all distraction and prepare themselves mentally to receive new information. The students should not only focus on what they are learning but visualize on how this information can be useful to them.

Student Activity:

- **Review** the assignment and identify the content you wish to retain

- **Write** down the book definition of the key concepts

- **Write** down your understanding of the concept based on the book interpretation

- **Visualize** by using your imagination and memory any lived experience that relates to the concept. How does this concept relate to you, your life? What is the closest association you have in your memory that you can identify this concept with?

- **Visualize** the content, and visualize how you see it applied in your life. See the concept working in your life. How is it operating? How is it beneficial? How can you use it to your advantage? If it is not working, why not? Visualize how you wish to see this information used in your life. Visualize why it is important for you to know more about it. Visualize retaining this information in your long-term memory. Visualize and see the trigger you will use to recall this information later. *It is important to not only visualize the concept working in your life, but feel what it feels like with all the emotions associated with it. Imagine that you are a higher facet of your own consciousness as you search for a memory that relates to the concept under study. By simple* **intent***, your desire to do it, you can find and merge with any appropriate memory to uncover your perception of that event, situation, issue or challenge to gain a deeper understanding of the concept and see how it operates and benefits you in your life, but more importantly you can manipulate as to how you would to see the end result.*

- **Recording visualizations**: After visualization, write down the lived experiences that surfaced that reflects or relates to the concept. Write down **how** and

why it relates to the concept. **Write** down the **trigger** that corresponds to the concept, and explain why you are using it. Take your time, reflect, contemplate and record all associated factors and emotions as related to the content for a deeper understanding and application of the contents relevance to your life. Writing things down is very important as the very act of writing reinforces information in human memories.

- After you have made and recorded the connection between content absorption (just understanding the content) to content connection (see applicability in your life), and have a memory trigger in place to retrieve the information when needed, spend a few extra minutes to further reinforce the memory by using creative visualization to imagine all the great benefits that you will have as a result of knowing this information. By utilizing creative visualization and expecting positive oucomes learning becomes fun and memorable, as it allows you to see the future possibilites of the new knowledge.

ACTIVITY 12 (FOR EDUCATOR)

GROUP LEP EDUCATOR PREPARATION CHECKLIST

Collaborative group work necessitates careful planning on the part of the educator and may be a challenge at times, but the rewards are significant as group work often leads to increased student engagement and learning outcomes. The educator as facilitator must direct the learning process and create an environment of trust as students will share personal information. Westberg and Jason (1996) offer a practical check list for educators of things to consider when creating group work that can be easily aligned with LEP teaching method to prepare for the group experience.

- Where does the LEP group experience fits into the overall curriculum?
- The group activities and the schedule—are the activities meaningful? Do they reflect LEP learning, and is there sufficient time to accomplish the goals?
- The planned group's size and mix of characteristics?
- Who the learners are—their interests, strengths, and learning needs?
- How decisions will be made in the group?
- How the learners will be evaluated?

BASIC STUDENT LEP IN-GROUP ACTIVITY

Small group work can be an important supplement to lectures, helping students' master concepts and apply them to material learned through the complex applications of their critical thinking skill, and LEP's inquisitive reflection.

In pair or groups discuss the book interpretation of the concept/s under discussion. Connect the concept to a lived experience from your life that reflects how that concept operates in your life. Why did you think of this particular lived experience when you thought of this concept? What attracted you to that lived experience when you thought of the concept? What triggered that memory? (The goal is to find out how the concept is understood and applies to each student, but also to address the group's collective understanding of the concept/s). Did each student in the group understand and interpret the concept in the same manner? Write your answers in the following table.

BASIC IN GROUP EXERCISE		
Topic:		
Learning Objective:		
CONCEPT/ TOPIC	**TEXT BOOK INTERPRETATION**	**LIVED EXPERIENCE**
Summary: Collective Group Understanding		

HELPFUL HANDOUT

LEP SIMPLE CONCEPT LEARNING MIND MAP

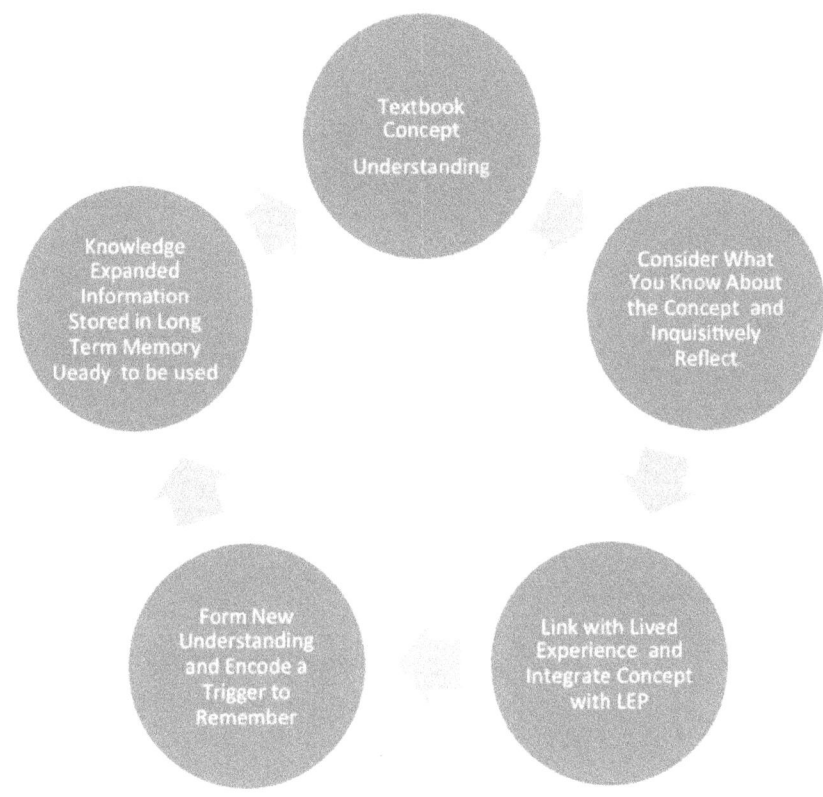

CHAPTER ELEVEN: Instructional Mind Mapping Activities and Helpful Handouts 121

REFERENCES

Abernathy, D. J. PreziQuote.com. Retrieved from https://prezi.com/9g-fkbs83b6z3/online-learning-is-not-the-next-big-thing-it-is-the-now-bi/

Aeschylus. BrainyQuote.com. Retrieved from https://www.brainyquote.com/search_results.html?q=%E2%80%9CMemory+is+the+mother+of+all+wisdom.%E2%80%9D++++

Ashford, S.J., & DeRue, D.S. (2012). Developing as a leader: The power of mindful engagement. *Organizational Dynamics, 41,* 146-154.

Astin, A. W. (1985). Involvement the cornerstone of excellence. *Change: The Magazine of Higher Learning, 17*(4).

Astin, A.W. (1984, July). Student involvement: A developmental theory for higher education. *Journal of College Student Personnel, 25*(4), 297-308.

Atwood, M. BrainyQuote.com. Retrieved from https://www.brainyquote.com/search_results.html?q=%E2%80%9CA+word+after+a+word+is+power.%E2%80%9D++.

Bahr, N., & Rohner, C. (2004). *The judicious utilization of new technologies through authentic learning in higher education: A case study.* Annual Conference Proceedings of Higher Education Research and Development Society of Australasia. Miki, Sarawak (Malaysia).

Baldwin, C. GoodReads.com quote. Retrieved from http://www.goodreads.com/quotes/103158-journal-writing-is-a-voyage-to-the-interior

Barkley, J. R. (2008, September). *Making sense of place according to lived experience.* University of Illinois at Urbana-Champaign.

Barkley, E. (2010). *Student engagement techniques: A handbook for college faculty.* San Francisco: Jossey-Bass.

Bartlett, F. C. (1932). *Remembering: An experimental and social study.* New York, NY: Cambridge University Press.

Bartlett, F.C. (1967). A theory of remembering. In F.C. Barton, *Remembering: A study in experimental and social psychology* (pp. 197-214). New York, NY: Cambridge University Press.

Barton, P. E. (2002). *Staying on course in education reform.* Princeton, NJ: Statistics & Research Division.

Bellon, J.J., Bellon, E.C. & Blank, M.A. (1991) *Teaching from a Research Knowledge Base: a Development and Renewal Process.* Facsimile edition. Upper Saddle, NJ: Prentice Hall

Bereiter, C., & Scardamalia, M. (1985). Cognitive coping strategies and the problem of inert knowledge. In S. F. Chipman, J. W. Segal, & R. Glaser. *Thinking and learning skills.* Hillside, NJ: Lawrence Erlbaum Associates.

Bhouraskar, S. (2017). *Teaching multicultural students.* Retrieved from Community for Accredited Online Schools http://www.accreditedschoolsonline.org/education-teaching-degree/multicultural-students/

Boud, D., Keogh, R., & Walker, D. (1985/1994). *Reflection: Turning experience into learning.* London: Kogan Page.

Bough, K. (2015). *Our brains are wired for stories.* Retrieved from http://www.definingstory.com/Bough-Strackbein-Brain-Story.pdf

Brown, M. N., & Kelley, S. M. (1986). *Asking the right questions: A guide to critical thinking.* Englewood Cliffs, NJ: Prentice Hall.

Bruster, B. & Peterson, B.R. (2012). Using critical incidents in teaching to promote reflective practice. *International and Multidisciplinary Perspectives, 14*(2).

Bryson, C., & Hand, L. (2007). The role of engagement in inspiring teaching and learning. *Innovations in Education and Teaching International, 44*(4), 349–363.

Buzan, T. YQuotes.com. Retrieved from http://yquotes.com/tony-buzan/23325/

Charner-Laird, K., Fiarman, S., Won Park, F., & Soderberg, S. (2003). *Cultivating student reflection.* Retrieved from http://ntpsmiddleschoolmath.wikispaces.com/file/view/Cultivating+Student+Reflection.pdf

Chen, Y.F. & Peng, S.S. (2008). University students internet use and its relationships with academic performance, interpersonal relationships, psychosocial adjustment, and self evaluation. *Cyber Psychology & Behavior 11*(4), 467-469.

Cherry, K. (2016). *What is problem solving?* Retrieved from https://www.verywell.com/what-is-problem-solving-2795485

Claxton, G. (2007). Expanding young people's capacity to learn. *British Journal of Educational Studies, 55*(2), 1–20.

CollegeAtlas, (2015). *College drop out statistics.* Retrieved from https://www.collegeatlas.org/college-dropout.html

Costa, A., & Kallick, B. (2008). *Learning and leading with habits of mind: 16 essential characteristics for success.* Alexandria, VA: ASCD Publishing.

Damasio, A. (2010). *Self comes to mind: Constructing a conscious brain.* New York, NY: Pantheon Books.

Delpit, L. (1998). What should teachers do? Ebonics and culturally responsive instruction. In T. Perry & L. Delpit (Eds.). *The real ebonics debate.* Boston, MA: Beacon Press.

Denzin, N.K. (1985). Emotion as lived experience. *Symbolic Interaction, 8*(2), 223-240.

Denzin, N.K. (1992). The many faces of emotionality. In Ellis and Flaherty (Eds.) *Investigating Subjectivity,* 17-30, Newbury Park, CA: Sage.

Denzin, N. (2001). *Interpretive interactionism.* Thousand Oaks, CA: Sage.

Dewey, J. (1964). *John Dewey on education: Selected writings* (R. D. Archambault, Ed.). Chicago: University of Chicago Press.

Dewey, J. (1933). *How we think.* New York: D. C. Heath.

Dewey, J. (1938). *Experience and education.* New York, NY: Collier Books.

Dilthey, W. (1985). *Poetry and experience.* Princeton, NJ: Princeton University Press.

Dole, S., Bloom, L., & Kowalske, K. (2016, April). Transforming pedagogy. *Interdisciplinary Journal of Problem-Based Learning, 10*(1).

Dostoevsky, F. Quote. Retrieved from http://quotationsbook.com/quote/25955/

Drucker, P. BrainyQuote.com. Retrieved from https://www.brainyquote.com/quotes/quotes/p/peterdruck120337.html

Dunn, R. (1997). The goals and track record of multicultural education. *Educational leadership: 54*(7), 74-77.

Ehrlich, T., & Fu, E. (2013). *Why college students need to self reflect.* Retrieved from http://www.forbes.com/sites/ehrlichfu/2013/08/15/why-college-students-need-to-self-reflect/#24b3eca66dd0

Eliot, T.S. BrainyQuote.com. Retrieved from https://www.brainyquote.com/quotes/quotes/t/tseliot101421.html

Einstein, A. GoodQuotes.com Retrieved from http://www.goodreads.com/quotes/6137386-education-is-not-the-learning-of-facts-but-the-training

Feuerstein, R. (with Rand, Y., Hoffman, M. B., & Miller, R.). (1980). *Instrumental enrichment: An intervention program for cognitive modifiability.* Baltimore, MD: University Park Press.

Fleming, N., & Baume, D. (2006, November). Learning styles again: VARKing up the right tree! *Educational Developments, 7*(4).

Fox, S. BrainyQuote.com. Retrieved from https://www.brainyquote.com/quotes/s/samanthafo431144.html

Franklin, B. BrainyQuote.com. Retrieved from https://www.brainyquote.com/quotes/quotes/b/benjaminfr383997.html

Fullan, M., & Langworthy, M. (2013). *Towards a new and: New pedagogies for deep learning.* Seattle, WA: Collaborative Impact.

Ginott, H. G. GoodreadsQuote.com. Retrieved from https://www.goodreads.com/author/quotes/212291.Haim_G_Ginott

Gonzales, N. & Moll, L. C. (2002). Cruzando el Puente: Building bridges to funds of knowledge. *Educational Policy 16*(4), 623-641.

Guskey, T.R. (2003, February). How classroom assessments improve learning. *Educational Leadership 60*(5), 6-11.

Harris, A.S., Bruster, B., Peterson, B. & Shutt, T. (2010). *Examining and facilitating reflection to improve professional practice.* New York, NY: Rowman & Littlefield.

Harris, L. R. (2008). A Phenomenographic investigation of teacher conceptions of student engagement in learning. *The Australian Educational Researcher, 5*(1), 57-79.

Heffernan, M. BrainyQuotes.com. Retrieved from https://www.brainyquote.com/quotes/quotes/m/margarethe556959.html

Hemming, H. E. (2000). Encouraging critical thinking: But...what does that mean? *Journal of Education, 35*(2), 173.

Hopper, C. (2015). *Practicing college learning strategies.* Boston, MA: Cengage.

Jakes, TD. Bishop. PurposefairyQuote.com. Retrieved from http://www.purposefairy.com/76444/there-is-nothing-as-powerful-as-a-changed-mind/

Joel, M. AZQuote.com. Retrieved from http://www.azquotes.com/quote/1499067

Johns, C. (2010). *Guided reflection: A narrative approach to advancing professional practice.* Singapore: Blackwell Publishing.

Kawasaki, G. AZQuotes.com. Retrieved from http://www.azquotes.com/quote/536784

Kemmis, S. (1985). Action research and the politics of reflection" in D. Boud, R. Keogh and D. Walker, (Eds). *Reflection: Turning experience into learning* (New York: Kogan Page Ltd., pp. 139 at 141.

Kifer, E. (2001). *Large-scale assessment: Dimensions, dilemmas, and policies.* Thousand Oaks, CA: Corwin Press.

Knefelkamp, L. (1997, Fall). Effective teaching for the multicultural classroom. *Diversity Digest. 2*(1), 11-12.

Kohn, A. AZ Quotes.com. Retrieved from http://www.azquotes.com/quote/728915'

Kohn, A. (2000). *The schools our children deserve: Moving beyond traditional classrooms and tougher standards.* New York, NY: First Houghton Mifflin.

Laal, M., & Laal, M. (2011). Collaborative learning: What is it? *Social and Behavioral Sciences 31,* 491–495.

Linn, R. L., & Miller, M.D. (2005). *Measurement and assessment in teaching.* Upper Saddle, NJ: Prentice Hall.

Looi, C. (2003). Cultural issues and the design of e-learning. *Proceedings of the First International Conference on Educational Technology in Cultural Context, 1*, 45- 59.

Lombardi, M. (2007, May). *Authentic learning for the 21st century: An overview.* Retrieved from https://net.educause.edu/ir/library/pdf/ELI3009.pdf

Manjusvara, (2005). *Writing your way.* Birmingham, England: Windhorse

Malcolm X. Quote. Retrieved fromhttp://stateofopportunity.michiganradio.org/post/classrooms-are-changing-and-students-need-teachers-who-are-ready-shift

Marchionini, G. (1995). *Information seeking in an electronic environment: Cambridge series on human computer interaction.* Cambridge, England: Cambridge University Press.

Marston, R.S. In P. McDaniel (Ed). *By the grace of God.* Raleigh, NC: Lulu Press.

McCarthy, K. BrainyQuote.com. Retrieved from https://www.brainyquote.com/quotes/quotes/k/kevinmccar721402.html

Meyer, J.H.F. & Land, R. (2005). The threshold concept and troublesome knowledge (2): epistemological considerations and a conceptual framework for teaching and learning, *Higher Education, 49*(3), 373-388.

Mezirow, J. (1990). How critical reflection triggers transformative learning. In J. Mezirow (Ed). *Fostering Critical Reflection in Adulthood* (pp. 1–20). San Francisco: Jossey-Bass Publishers.

Mezirow, J. (1991). *Transformative dimensions in adult learning.* San Francisco: Jossey-Bass Publishers.

Mezirow, J. (1996). Contemporary paradigms of learning. *Adult Education Quarterly, 46(3), 158–172.*

Miller, G. (1956). The magical number seven, plus or minus two: Some limits on our capacity for processing information. *The Psychological Review, 63*, 81–97.

Moses, B. (1982). Visualization: A different approach to problem solving. *School of Science and Mathematics, 82*(2), 141-147.

Morrison, B. AZQuote.com. Retrieved from http://www.azquotes.com/quote/542004

Nextthought, (2016, January, 20). *Adding a personal touch to online design learning.* Retrieved from https://nextthought.com/thoughts/2016/01/adding-a-personal-touch-to-online-learning-design

Norman, D. (1993). *Things that make us smart.* New York: Diversion Books.

North, A. C., Hargreaves, D. J., McKendrick, J. (1999, April). The influence of in-store music on wine selections. *Journal of Applied Psychology, 84*(2), 271-276. http://dx.doi.org/10.1037/0021-9010.84.2.271

Ocholla-Ayayo, A.B.C. (1976). 1980. *The Luo culture: a reconstruction of the material patterns of a traditional African society.* Wiesbaden, Germany: Steiner.

Olneck, M. R. (1995). Immigrants and education. In J.A. Banks & C.A.M Banks (Eds.). *Handbook of research on multicultural education*. New York: Macmillan.

Ormrod, J. E. & Rice, F. P. (2003). *Lifespan development and learning*. Boston, MA: Pearson.

Pahomov, L. (2014). *Authentic learning in the digital age*. Alexandria, VA: ASCD.

Palloff, R. M., & Pratt, K. (2005). *Collaborating online: Learning together in community*. San Francisco, CA: Jossey-Bass.

Pavlov, I. P. (1897). *The work of the digestive glands*. London, England: Griffin.

Pink, D. H. (2005). *A whole new mind*. New York, NY: Penguin Books.

Pink, D. H. (2006). *A whole new mind*. New York, NY: Penguin Books.

Polya, G. (1957). *How to solve it*. Princeton, NJ: Princeton University Press.

Pulliam, K.K. BrainyQuote.com Retrieved from https://www.brainyquote.com/quotes/quotes/k/keshiaknig565640.html

Sanders, W.L., & Rivers, J.C. (1996). *Cumulative and residual effects of teachers on future student academic achievement*. Research Progress Report. Knoxville: University of Tennessee Value-Added Research and Assessment Center.

Sartre, J.P. (1985). *Existentialism and human emotions*. New York: Citadel Press.

Sawyer, B. (2003, November). *Authenticity, the self, and philosophy as reflection*. Retrieved from https://briansawyer.net/2003/11/18/chapter-2-authenticity-the-self-and-philosophy-as-reflection/

Schutz, A. (1967). *Studies in social theory: Collected papers, II*. The Hague: Martinus Nijhoff.

Scriven, M., & Paul, R. (1996). *Defining critical thinking: A draft statement for the National Council for Excellence in Critical Thinking*. Retrieved from http://www.criticalthinking.org/pages/defining-critical-thinking/766

Sen, A. (2004). How does culture matter? In Rao, V., & Walton, M. (Eds.) *Culture and public action*. CA: Stanford University Press.

Shakirova, D.M. (2007). Technology for the shaping of college students' and upper-grade students' critical thinking. *Russian Education Society, 49*(9), 42-52.

Shattuck, S. (2016, April, 29). The four different types of learnings, and what they mean to your Presentations [Web log post]. Retrieved from https://blog.prezi.com/the-four-different-types-of-learners-and-what-they-mean-to-your-presentations-infographic/

Solms, M. & Turnbull, O. (2002). *The brain and the inner world*. London, England: Karnac

Sonoma State University Center for Critical Thinking, (2015). *Teachers of teachers: Examining preparation for critical thinking*. Retrieved from http://www.criticalthinking.org/pages/center-for-critical-thinking/401

Sparrow, B., Liu, J., & Wegner, D. M. (2011). *Google effects on memory: Cognitive consequences of having information at our fingertips*. Web of Science Magazine. Retrieved from http://psychology.ua.edu/wp-content/uploads/2016/03/Google-Is-Changing-the-Way-we-Think.pdf

Sprenger, M. (1999). *Learning and memory: The brain in action*. Alexandria, VA: ASCD.

Standage, T. (2012, January/February). Writing is the greatest invention. *Intelligent Life Magazine.*

Tarbell, I. BrainyQuote.com. Retrieved from https://www.brainyquote.com/search_results.html?q=%E2%80%98%E2%80%9CImagination+is+the+only+key+to+the+future.+Without+it%2C+none+exists.+With+it+all+things+are+possible.%E2%80%9D+

Totten, S., Sills, T., Digby, A., & Russ, P. (1991). *Cooperative learning: A guide to research* . New York: Garland.

Turner, Mark. (1996). The literary mind: *The origins of thought and language*. Oxford, England: Oxford University Press.

United States Dept. of Labor, Bureau of Labor Statistics, (2016). Retrieved from https://www.bls.gov/

University of Illinois, (2017). *Instructional strategies for online courses*. Illinois Online Network. Retrieved from http://www.ion.uillinois.edu/resources/tutorials/pedagogy/instructionalstrategies.asp

University of Pittsburgh, Department of Communication, (2007). *Teaching oral communications: A few basics*. Retrieved from www.speaking.pitt.edu

University of Reading, (2017). *Why is feedback important?* Retrieved from http://www.reading.ac.uk/internal/engageinfeedback/Whyisfeedbackimportant/

Valli, L. *(1997).* Listening to other voices: A description of teacher reflection in the United States. *Peabody Journal of Education, 72*(1), 67-88.

Van Doren, M. Brainy Quote.com. Retrieved from https://www.brainyquote.com/search_results.html?q=The+art+of+teaching+is+the+art+of+assisting+discovery.%E2%80%9D

Walshe, R. D. (1987). The learning power of writing. *The English Journal, 76*(6), 22-27.

Wheatley, M. J. BrainyQuote.com Retrieved from https://www.brainyquote.com/quotes/quotes/m/margaretj283925.html

Wilczynski, E. (2009, November, 20). *Teaching basic communication skills*. Retrieved from www.seenmagazine.us

Yorke, M. (2002) Academic failure: A retrospective view from non-completeing students. In: *Failing students in higher education* (Eds Peelo, M & Wareham, T Maindenhead, Berskshire: SRHE and Open University Press.

Yost, D.S., & Forlenza-Bailey, A.M. (2000). The Impact of a fifth year program on the leadership abilities of beginning teachers. *The Professional Educator, 23*(1).

Zygouris-Coe, V. (2012). *Proceedings from ICITE 2012: Collaborative learning in an online teacher education course: Lessons earned.* Retrieved from http://www.icicte.org/Proceedings2012/Papers/08-4-Zygouris-Coe.pdf

www.ingramcontent.com/pod-product-compliance
Lightning Source LLC
Chambersburg PA
CBHW070945230426
43666CB00011B/2570